THE JUDAS

The Judas Window

FELICITY BIELOVICH

First printing: July 1996

Published by Zoetic Inc.
6370 Chatham Street, West Vancouver, British Columbia
V7W 2E2, Canada

ISBN 0-9697551-2-0

Distributed in Southern Africa by Southern Book Publishers (Pty) Ltd.
P.O. Box 3103
Halfway House 1685
South Africa

Printed in Canada by Best Gagne Book Manufacturers.

ACKNOWLEDGEMENTS

Every book has a history, and mine is no different. For making it possible I have acclaimed author John Kehoe to thank. It was he who sowed the seed for the *Judas Window* over lunch one hot Friday afternoon in a Johannesburg bistro. South African editor Jeremy Wightman, a very likeable and intelligent young man, nurtured it to the transplant stage; whereupon it travelled all the way to my editors in Canada, Ric and Jennifer Beairsto, who saw it through to maturity. Although continents divide us, they have become friends, and for having accompanied and encouraged me throughout my journey, and for capturing the spirit of my story with such empathy and penetrating insight, I salute them. When I first saw the cover design by Jenny Dozel, it literally took my breath away, brilliantly depicting for me the reality and horror of being "put away." For setting me free from guilt and giving me the most lucid explanation of what benzodiazepines could and did do to me, I have Charles Medawar and his riveting and definitive book, *Power and Dependence,* to thank. Likewise with Will Day, Australian benzodiazepine researcher who provided me with the Minutes of the 1994 Benzodiazepine Conference, opening the door for me to make contact with distinguished benzodiazepine expert Malcolm Lader, Professor of Clinical Psychopharmacology in London, as well as many others in the field. And finally to my God and the big five: Nicky, Elizabeth, Cathy, Linda and Debby, who encouraged me with laughter and tears to "go tell it on the mountain," my enduring love and gratitude.

CONTENTS

This is the Hour of Lead—
Remembered, if outlived,
As freezing persons, recollect the Snow—
First—Chill—then Stupor—then the letting go—

Emily Dickinson (1830–1894)

CHAPTER ONE

When Winter Reigns

I know the countdown has begun the moment I enter the dressmaker's shop. I'm there with my daughter Deborah to collect her debutante's dress, and seeing the mass of frothy white tulle and organza elegantly draped over the red velvet chaise lounge, something inside me suddenly begins to scream, "Get out of this shop now! Run, Felicity, run and never come back!" Blind terror engulfs me, terror that seizes and penetrates my core, leaving me helpless, vulnerable, paralysed. My eyes dart about looking at everything, nothing, avoiding eye contact. My hands shake. My whole body quakes. Debby picks up the dress, hugs it to herself and swirls around on the well-worn Persian carpet squealing in delight, "Isn't it just too beautiful, Mom?" I want to scream, "Leave me alone, don't talk to me! I'm not here! I don't know where the hell I am!" But with great effort I somehow manage a, "Yes it is, Debs." My voice sounds hollow, distant. All I can hear clearly is the clickety-clack, clickety-clack of the passing train chanting to me, "Jump in front. Jump in front." I grit my teeth, take a deep breath and tell myself, "Just a few more minutes and you'll get your pills. Your pills."

Debby leaves the shop with a spring in her step, oblivious to what is happening to me. We drive home with her chattering in the passenger seat and me feverishly gripping the steering wheel, fighting the clickety-clack the entire way.

I close the front door behind me, literally run down the passage and grab my pills. Water trickles down my chin as I greedily gulp them down. "Give them time," I agitatedly tell myself, "give them time." The doorbell rings. "Answer it please, Mom, I'm trying my dress on," calls Debby from her bedroom. I step back down the passage, look out my sewing-room window, and my heart leaps in alarm. It's Helen and Margaret, my two sisters-in-law. I can't possibly face them right now. Clickety-clack. Clickety-clack, goes the train. "Pull yourself together, Felicity. You'll be fine," I tell myself, not at all convinced but grasping at anything until the pills can take effect. They move into the family-room and sit down. Helen looks at me strangely. I can see by her face that she knows something's terribly wrong with me. I force myself to make small-talk. "Tomorrow is Debby's big night," I say woodenly. Clickety-clack. Clickety-clack. I just wish they'd go and leave me. There is some kind of terrible "movement" happening inside my head and I can't understand why. I feel like a cornered animal.

My back is to the door as Debby enters the living room. "Oh, you look beautiful, Debs," says Margaret. I turn to Debby and my heart misses a beat. She looks so innocent and vulnerable. I love her so much. She waves the crimson ostrich feather she will carry and comes and curtseys in front of me. Her magnificent blue eyes are as clear as the sky. "Jump in front. Jump in front," goes the clickety-clack. Tautening every fibre in my body, I will myself to say, "You look beautiful, my angel." Hoping Helen and Margaret will get the message I add, "If we're to eat before we go to the rehearsal, you'd better hurry up." Mercifully, they stand up and move toward the door. Clickety-clack, clickety-clack.

Fate was kind to me the night I met Nicky Bielovich on a school dance-floor. I had just turned seventeen and he was a distinguished-looking young man in a Christian Brothers College old boys blazer. His height was average; his hair already receding at the temples. Large brown eyes drew me to him like a magnet. In a very short time my heart had been captured by his gentlemanly ways, placid nature, and sheer goodness. Our courtship spanned three wonderful, carefree years. We danced, played tennis, listened to music, went to the movies, the theatre, dined out, and did a tremendous amount of talking. He was a butcher by trade and worked for his father. We spoke endlessly about our Croatian, Irish and English roots—how they influenced us, what they meant. Both of us wanted to return to them some day. The night he raised the topic of children, I was elated to discover that he, like me, wanted four. The coincidence was not so surprising given that we were both raised in large families; he was the eldest of four, I the youngest of five. I was determined to have all four children before I turned thirty, and he must have sensed my urgency. He proposed that same night, and I accepted. Three months later, with great fanfare, my father walked me down the aisle of the same Catholic church that both Nicky and I had been baptized in as children. Looking back, marrying Nicky was the best thing I ever did. It probably saved my life.

He was a fast mover, my Nicky. With a straight flush, he gave me four beautiful daughters—Elizabeth, Catherine, Linda and Deborah—and beat my age thirty deadline by two years. I settled into the role of housewife with ease. For South African women in the early sixties this was still the norm. I nursed our little brood through their childhood illnesses, head stitchings, fractures and plaster casts with love and patience. Year after year I happily bounced them along in my Datsun 1200 to school, athletics, dancing, swimming and art lessons. As a family we played hard and worked hard.

My children came with me to the outskirts of town where I was helping to revamp the mission school, where they saw for themselves the ugly reality of "separate development," as it was then called. The school was a shabby building with broken windows, paint peeling from the walls, a handful of desks, and a concrete floor that turned feet icy in winter. Nicky and I picked up desks from convents that were closing down, loaded them into our truck at 5 a.m., and delivered them to the school. We painted the walls, hung pelmets, made curtains, begged for floor tiles, and did what we could to ease a deplorable situation. Our efforts were short-lived, however, and it was a sad day for the township when the government introduced its Bantu Education Bill, withdrew its subsidy, and people too poor to carry the burden alone watched their school pulled down.

Through these years I always had a busy circle of friends and associates. And yet my centre was always my family, including the extended family. Grandparents, uncles, aunts, nieces, nephews, everyone was within the inner circle. In this way Nicky and I established our traditions, discovered our values and imprinted for everyone lasting memories of family get-togethers. We worked as a team, raising our children by trial and error, and doing it our own way. Aged maxims like "children are to be seen and not heard" and "speak only when you are spoken to" had no place in our home. Our children learned something we had not—to question, to analyse, to criticize constructively. To sit at our supper table was to see democracy in action—everyone equal, everyone with a chance to have their say. No special privileges for the eldest; no exceptions made for the youngest. Sitting at our table I loved to listen to my daughters' childish banter, hear the opinions, watch their interplay at work, to see their reaction when they lost an argument, won a victory.

One year, after Nicky followed my father's advice and invested in sugar shares, the price of the shares jumped so high we were able to afford a second honeymoon. We toured England, Ireland, Croatia and Europe, exploring our roots and thoroughly enjoying ourselves.

These were glorious times. I savoured life. I was in charge. Nothing seemed impossible to me, least of all pulling out the roots of an old palm tree we had recently cut down. The gardener we employed to do this obviously didn't understand my time-frame. All he needed, it seemed to me, was a quick lesson in what just a little effort could do.

Load and throw, load and throw. A vigorous demonstration of how to shovel and throw a load of sand over the shoulder in one sweeping arc. But then searing pain tears into my back and sends me reeling to the ground. I am carried inside. The doctor arrives and I am ordered to take a week's bed rest.

But a little back pain can't keep me down. The next week I resume my hectic pace. Only when I can barely stand, walk, or get up in the morning do I admit to myself that there must be something seriously wrong. My years of bounty are over. A decade of doctors is about to begin.

My first impression of Dr. Jeffrey is that he belongs in the movies. He has it all—the height, the looks, the body, the voice. He even has the big feet that I like to see on a man. He is at the peak of his career and is recognized internationally as one of the top ten orthopaedic surgeons in the world. As Nicky and I sit down he opens the conversation on a light-hearted note: "I see in Felicity's file that you're a butcher, Nicky. I'm very interested to find out more about how a butcher cuts through joints and muscles and removes the bone. I'd love to have a chat with you some time. In a sense, we're in the same job. Only I have to keep my patients alive." He and Nicky continue their conversation about beef and bones for a moment, before he turns to me. "Right Felicity, where is the pain? Tell me what happened to you?"

Dr. Jeffrey writes down my history, calls for X-rays, reads them and hospitalizes me for a myelogram there and then. (A myelogram is a procedure where dye is injected into the spinal cavity in order to show what the normal X-ray cannot.) He explains how removal of the laminae (which form a major part of the vertebral arch) will solve my problem.

If one wants a foretaste of hell, this procedure would be the way to go. But the travails of the operation itself pale into insignificance when compared to the immediate aftermath of the surgery. Forks of lightning strike every nerve in the lower region of my spine each time the nursing staff arrive at my bed to turn me. Nevertheless, they carry out Dr. Jeffrey's meticulous orders to the letter, and in six weeks I am back on my feet, as if nothing had ever happened.

Eleven months later I am convening a school bazaar. As usual I take on the work of six. I drive the truck, load the steel tables, climb, cart and carry. I churn out aprons, peg bags, tea towels and night-dresses by the dozens. But this pace can't continue. Something has to give. Something does—my back. Debilitating pain and numbness in my legs drive me back to Dr. Jeffrey. This time the myelogram reveals an unstable spine, and he advises I undergo a spinal fusion. This is major surgery. It involves an incision running from above the navel down to the pubic bone. A piece of hip bone is removed to fuse the three lumbar vertebra with, and four vanadium screws are inserted.

Given the seriousness of the operation, I go for a second opinion, driving to a teaching hospital to consult with an eminent professor. Both his appearance and manner are totally opposite to that of Dr. Jeffrey. He has a flat, bald head and small brown eyes; what he lacks in height he makes up in width. Pompous, cold and rude throughout the consultation, which is conducted in the company of his equally rude students, he nevertheless arrives at the same conclusion: a spinal fusion is imperative. Dr. Jeffrey performs the operation on my daughter Elizabeth's sixteenth birthday.

Once again the pain which ensues from the operation is nearly indescribable. Only Nicky's gentle touch, and the golden smiles from the girls when they visit at the clinic each day, keep me from letting the torment overwhelm me. I struggle to find hope in little things. One morning a bird resting on the windowsill to fluff its feathers uplifts me. Another time it is the glorious jacaranda tree blooming outside my window. Nowhere in the world are they as beautiful as in South Africa, especially in the summer after a rain, when you can smell everything so distinctly, even through a hospital window. And I repeat my mother's mantra—"Every day, in every way, I am getting better and better." I also find encouragement in the visits from the Croatian priest whom I meet on his ward rounds the day after my operation.

The day before I leave the clinic, Dr. Jeffrey mentions, for the first time, that I will be encased in a fibreglass cast from under my armpits to below my left knee. I'm stunned, very distraught, and he pats me on the arm saying, "If I had told you, Felicity, you would have run a mile. Take my advice, put a pillow on your stomach and start reading. Mark the days off on a calendar. They'll fly. And don't put on any weight. I'll see you in another fourteen weeks." Before he leaves the room I want to know why my left knee is to be included in the cast and he laughs, "I've had women who have wiggled themselves to the bathroom and undone all my good work. I won't let this happen with you."

Creating the cast involves my standing stark naked while a young man slides a cheesecloth tube over my body down to my buttocks, likewise from thigh to below the knee. This is to protect the cast from scratching. As if winding up a bobbin, he then wraps me in wet bandages. When he is done I step into a drying machine. When he opens it I am mummified. I feel entombed, beached on my bed like a dying whale. I am only able to move one leg and both my arms. It is impossible for me to turn myself. (I need someone to help me do this every two to three hours.) My head has a fifteen centimetre lifting capability, and can turn from side to side.

Home I go with a sheepskin for my back, Agiolax for my bowels and elastic stockings for my legs. No one mentions the thing I will need most of all—the bedpan. If one is to become user-friendly and avoid neurosis, there are certain things one needs to know about bedpans. I know nothing. This taints our relationship right from the start. I am, for instance, unaware that the bedpan comes in different shapes. Nicky returns from the chemist with a selection of three, but

I have no idea as to the merits of the "flat-bottomed," "lipped" or "slipper" version. I just want to use one—desperately. It might be amusing for someone else to watch Nicky struggle, push, lift, grunt and swear as he valiantly tries to shove the bedpan under the cast, but for me it is no laughing matter. Meal times are another travail. I scoop food into my mouth with a spoon, drink through a straw and constantly mess my pillowcase.

A daytime nurse is hired, and Nicky takes the night shift. This means a bed-bath, a change of nightdress, foot massage and bedpan session. While he does this, I scratch myself under the plaster with a knitting needle and mark another day off the calendar. Whenever I thank him for his kindness, because he never once complains, he reminds me of our wedding vows, "In sickness or in health." The girls in turn mother him. They learn to cook, bake and keep house. I grow to love the smell of the aromatic vapours floating down the passage, the sound of laughter coming from the TV room. These sensations reassure me that life is still moving forward. And this notion is reinforced whenever the parish or Croatian priest comes to the house and offers Mass in my bedroom. Afterwards everyone stays in the room for a picnic supper, served by the girls. This is family life at its best.

My time in bed is well spent. I read, write letters, play tapes and run up a huge telephone account. Family and friends are fantastic. They visit regularly and bring gifts and beautifully prepared meals. Sometimes I envy them and their freedom. I would also like to look as good as they do, wear something other than a nightdress, go out for dinner. Nevertheless, because of all the support, I remain cheerful and never become depressed. Nor do I ever resort to drugs of any sort, not even pain-killers. I'm sure I'll soon be one hundred percent again.

The last week lying in the cast is the most difficult. I am impatient to walk, take a real bath, eat a meal in the dining room, see my garden. Above all I want to part company with the loathsome bedpan. We never do become friends. Finally the day arrives, the cast is sawn off and I am taken, still supine, to the plaster room to have a mould taken for the brace I will wear for the next six weeks. In the doorway stands the same young man who'd earlier wound me like a bobbin. "Glad to see you're back," he says with a smile. "Today's your big day. Up you get." My feet touch the ground. But after fourteen weeks without any real exercise my muscles are extremely weak. My head swims. I faint dead away.

More trauma follows when the Croatian priest arrives that same day to say that my father is in critical condition in a nearby hospital. Nicky takes me to see him. I refuse to go into his room in a wheelchair. I want him to see me walk. And he does, with a little help from Nicky. I only stay a few minutes.

The priest is right; my father is dying. The entire weekend Nicky carts me back and forth to the hospital; en route I lie on a mattress in the back of a borrowed station-wagon. The first time in four months that I wear clothes is to my father's funeral three days later. I lie on a mattress in the side chapel. The fact that I'm physically unable to help my mother in her time of sorrow multiplies my grief.

I take very good care of myself after this, going for regular checkups and getting stronger all the time. Before long, for the first time in years, I bask in good health. As before, I take part in all the girls' activities, with all of my old enthusiasm. I attend a school sports meet where Linda is running in the four-hundred metres. As she rounds the final turn, emerging to take the lead, I get so excited, jumping and shouting, that I lose my footing and fall off the grandstand, landing heavily on my tailbone. Within two days I know I'm again in trouble. I can't sit without excruciating pain.

Reluctantly, once again I return to Dr. Jeffrey. I've broken my coccyx, and the ensuing operation removes any remaining vestige of pride. Now, wherever I go I travel with both a cushion and a globe chair with a hole cut in the middle. Eight weeks later, Dr. Jeffrey gives me the all clear. In parting he says to me, "You've been one helluva patient, Felicity, the way you've kept bouncing back. But listen, enough is enough. I never want to see you here again." He never does.

Once again I am back on the wheel of life—a fast wheel. Everything is popping in the Bielovich household. There are matric dance dresses to make, farewell parties to organize. Boyfriends come onto the scene, and Nicky welcomes them with open arms. Elizabeth is off to university, and Cathy is off to teachers' training college. They both happily take up residence away from home, and suddenly new horizons are opening up for me. For the first time in twelve years I am going to have some time of my own. My very own! I look forward to it.

And then the twinges start. Just a little pain down one leg, an odd stab of pain shooting upwards to where my coccyx had been, a pain in the lumbar region where my spine has been fused. "You've stood too long, not sat right, done too much. Do more exercises," I tell myself, trying to ignore the pain. But it continues. It centres mostly in my pelvis, so I consult a gynaecologist. He puts it all down to a lack of hormones and pumps me full of them. The pain becomes excruciating, crippling. Finally, he suggests I go to an orthopaedic surgeon. I am desperate enough to agree.

Back to Dr. Jeffrey's office, but on my arrival, I discover he has left the country for an indefinite period. Devastated, I phone his anaesthetist for a recommendation and am referred to a Dr. Royston.

It is a freezing cold morning when I first meet Dr. Royston. The moment I open the door he apologizes for the beret on his head. "It's getting thin on top and I'm beginning to feel it," he says. He has twinkling eyes, a trim moustache and long, bony fingers. "You've got an ugly history here, Mrs. Bielovich," he comments, grimacing while looking at my file. "But try not to worry before we have the X-rays. I'll ask the radiologist to hurry you along." I like him already; something about his manner puts me at ease.

Turning away from the light box, Dr. Royston's face is grave. He walks round the desk, places his hand gently on my shoulder, "Mrs. Bielovich, I'm terribly, terribly sorry to have to say this, but you need a pelvic fusion without delay." I am stunned, then ashamed. "How am I ever going to tell the family?" I think. "They must be sick of having a mother always in bed, always dependent." My thoughts are interrupted by Dr. Royston, concern evident in his voice: "Is there anything I can do for you, Mrs. Bielovich? Are you able to drive yourself home? Would you like me to phone someone to come for you?" He calls the receptionist in and orders me a cup of tea. I simply don't have the will to go home and tell the family. I am sick of having to be nursed. I drive to a nearby church and ask God, Why?

To reach the sacro-iliac joints the surgeon cuts a crescent from below the waistline down into each buttock. The pain isn't anywhere near as severe as with the spinal fusion, but it does involve seven weeks flat on my back. Dr. Royston wins my lifetime gratitude by making a concession with regard to the bedpan. If I am accompanied and wear a harness, I can walk the five metres to my bathroom three times in a twenty-four-hour period. Wonderful as this sounds to me initially, the reality is rather more sobering. The harness weighs four kilograms. It comprises two parallel steel bars, from shoulder to waist, for the vertebra to snuggle into, with straps going over the shoulders down to the thigh and into a corset with threaded eyelets. Rivetted to the vertebral bars are two circular bands of steel, one around the hip bones, the other tightly around the lower pelvis. These bands have to be pried open for me to manoeuvre myself into while lying down, a process that in itself takes several minutes to complete.

Nevertheless, because I can go to the bathroom, I choose not to have a day nurse. A maid comes twice weekly. The other days, when the girls are at school, I am entirely on my own in the house. Visiting family members and friends get around this without any problem. I keep the front door key on a long stick. They come to the window and collect it, letting themselves in and out. If I need to use the bedpan I phone Nicky at the abattoir or the shop. The mood he finds me in is dependent on how quickly he arrives.

My time in bed pays off. X-rays show a perfect fusion. However, it doesn't take me long to realize that this convalescence isn't following my previous pattern. I can't stand or sit for long. I attribute this to general weakness, but the pain reaches the point where I feel I am plugged into an open socket. The pain centres between my legs, and I find this too embarrassing to speak about. I become agitated, restless and very, very frightened at the thought of more surgery. I speak to our family doctor about it. He believes it has something to do with the nerve ends of the spine, and makes an appointment for me with a leading neurologist.

Dr. Grant is an Oxford man, intelligent looking, immaculately dressed—Saville Row no doubt—somewhere in his thirties. He conducts a battery of nerve tests, followed by an electro-encephalograph. It appears that some of my nerve ends are badly inflamed, while others could be entrapped in scar tissue. He commences sleep-therapy, via an intravenous drip, that very night. Whatever is in that drip keeps me semicomatose for a fortnight. When I finally leave the clinic, for the first time, I am armed with bottles of pills to keep the pain, now considerably reduced, under control. Little do I know or understand that this is the beginning of a nightmare that will change the entire course of my life.

Each time I feel the red-hot pokerlike pain penetrate my pelvis, I take my pills. Each time every nerve in my body screams, "I can't take it anymore," I take my pills, as prescribed. They make me dizzy, give me a thick muzzy feeling in my head. I cry over nothing, have panic attacks. My moods change. But still I take my pills, following exactly the doctor's instructions. And soon these pills become my crutch.

I return to the neurologist on a monthly basis for a check-up, and am always honest with him, telling him exactly what I'm feeling. He appears interested and concerned. Each time I am sent off for an EEG and more nerve-monitoring tests. The outcome is always the same—more pills. "I want you to try these until I see you next month. Remember, you can always call me." I do, even at his house. "Dr. Grant, there's something funny going on inside my head. I can't stop thinking. My hands are shaking. I can't stop crying. What must I do?" His usual response is, "Don't worry about it. It will settle down. Do you still have some of the . . . ? Take one of those. Increase the. . . . Reduce the. . . . Come and see me next week." I always do. As a result my medication becomes a bewildering series of different cocktails. My symptoms vary accordingly.

One night I call Dr. Grant at home, crying hysterically, "I can't take the constant mood swings! I need help!" He suggests that the problem might be hormonal. Back to the gynaecologist. "He could be right," says Dr. Kogan, a rotund little man. I am already on oral hormone replacement therapy, so he introduces oestrogen injections fortnightly. My prolactin count soars. (Prolactin is a hormone which causes lactation in a woman.) Parlodel, a tablet used to dry up milk in nursing mothers, is prescribed to combat this and "balance" everything out. More and more blood tests are conducted. I am called back to Dr. Kogan's office. "You need a brain scan. Your blood results indicate there could be a tumour on the pituitary." Again I am stunned, and again I can't bring myself to tell the family. I have the scan without their knowing, and it's negative. But Dr. Kogan is still unhappy. "Your count is far too high for there to be nothing. I want you to go for another scan in a fortnight." A curt phone call from a laboratory assistant the day before I go for the second scan informs me, "We made a mistake with one of the noughts." No further scan is necessary. I must simply stay on the Parlodel.

I had always been prone to headaches, but now they are so severe that the doctor calls at the house to give me pethadene injections. These knock me out for a couple of hours, and leave me with a thick-headed hangover when I arise. My moods switch channels by the hour. My usually good sleeping pattern is erratic, disturbed by profuse sweats. I feel an empty hole in the pit of my stomach, an inexplicable anxiety. Once again Dr. Kogan puts this down to a hormonal imbalance. "It's quite natural at your age. Lots of women get panicky during change of life. It's called midlife crisis." Strange as it may seem, my spirits are lifted by this pronouncement. My crazy feelings have a name. I can fight it like I had the operations. I stick to the doctor's instructions.

The thought of the brightly coloured "jelly-babies" waiting at my bedside helps me get through each day. I take these "babies" in the bath, and I am now on twelve to fifteen pills a day: diazepam, oxazepam, lorazepam, temazepam, bromazepam, nitrazepam, triazolam, flunitrazepam (see Appendix). Soon an ever-changing selection of antidepressants is added to the mix. They are not all taken simultaneously, but in combinations determined and prescribed by the neurologist.

Each night, the fast-track slows by the time I crawl into bed, and Morpheus welcomes me to limbo for a few hours. But I curse the dawn. It means I have to be up and doing. And it means another sweep into a terrifying territory I have never been into before—the darkest recesses of my mind. Each day I feel as though I'm slowly becoming a stranger, even unto myself.

Nevertheless, up until this point, I am still relatively in charge. I cry copiously in the morning, but not until the girls are at school. I lie on the bed whenever I can, but throw meals together at the last minute to make it look as if I have been busy all day. I continue to visit my mother, with whom I've always enjoyed a very close relationship. She has the charm of the Irish and the wisdom of Solomon, and we are the best of friends. Often she says to me when we're returning from our sewing circle or some other function, "Darling, what's come over you? You're not listening when people talk. You're always fidgeting and going off to the bathroom. What's bothering you?" Normally she is very easy to talk to, but when I tell her I think I am going crazy she can only reply, "I don't understand all this change of life business. Nor do I like all the pills you are taking."

"But Mommy," I reply, "the doctor says that the pills will eventually cure me."

"Forget what the doctor says, Felicity, stop the Parlodel." She truly believes that it is this particular pill which is causing my problem.

I speak to Elizabeth and her fiancé, George, about what mother has said. George is a fourth-year dental student, and he rattles me further by essentially agreeing with my mother. "Mrs. B," he says, sitting on a windowsill with Elizabeth at his side, "I think it's all the tablets that are to blame for how you're feeling. Take a look at what happens to the brain when you take benzodiazepines (tranquillizers)." He draws a diagram of the brain, tries to explain synapses, receptors, the limbic system, but I don't have a clue about what he is saying. I pretend to listen but think to myself, "What does he know? He's not a doctor. How can pills possibly change a personality so much? It has to be something wrong with *me*." Why else would I no longer remember where I parked the car, what I went shopping for or what I bought? Why do I want to tell everybody to go to hell, leave me alone? Why, when Nicky and the girls look at me, do I want to bury my face in my hands? Why do I want to hide away, be buried in a deep hole? I have no answers and this only confirms my worst fear: I am indeed going crazy. I go to see the Catholic priest and tell him the devil is taking over.

Whenever I get behind the wheel of the car on an open road I don't know what comes over me. I push the car to its limits. Every horse in the engine seems to know exactly what I want from it, and responds accordingly. So do the tires; they stick to the road like chewing gum. I have the timing and skill of a Formula One veteran as I weave in and out of peak traffic. Coming up rapidly behind a driver, I hug his exhaust pipe and Morse-code a defiant message with my lights. Invariably he gives way. The rude gestures, angry faces, flashing lights which register in my rear-view mirror only super-charge my flow of adrenaline. I watch the needle climb to 180 kilometres per hour, knowing that if I press down hard enough on the accelerator I will fly. The experience leaves me almost breathless. Never feeling the slightest element of danger, I watch the landmarks disappear so fast that I often overshoot my off-ramp.

Following in the wake of a speeding ambulance at dusk one day, adrenaline pumping, head humming, radio blaring, I find I have entered an enormous unknown black township. Normally this would frighten me, but, feeling godlike, I swing the steering wheel sharply to the right, and climb the verge. In the process I nearly wipe out a group of young men waiting for a bus. Undeterred, I leave them wildly gesticulating in the dust and hurtle back onto the highway. I am invincible.

All areas of my life are becoming increasingly disturbed, erratic and fragmented. My vision is blurred; people's voices come in and out of my head like waves on a beach. I am unravelling like a ball of string. And the more I find myself being sucked into myself, the more I run to the bathroom to take my jelly-babies.

One afternoon, to prove to myself that I am still normal, I undertake to type Elizabeth's thesis. The effort quickly becomes a nightmare. Nothing I type makes any sense. I can't concentrate, focus, separate or still the thoughts that are tearing around my "cracking" head. I type at the dining-room table, oblivious to everything around me. I type without commas or full stops. I type and I type, because as long as I sit in front of the machine and type I can tell myself I am coping.

My typing also helps me deal with these deep-seated urges to jump in front of the four-minutes-past-five train which surfaces at the edge of my mind at regular intervals with a clickety-clack, clickety-clack. When it does, I break out into a sweat, and I'm gripped by a savage fear which threatens to engulf me. Type, Felicity, type, type, type. *If you don't, your head is going to crack open like an egg, and the slimy part is going to run out.*

My struggle is in vain. The slime oozes. I am losing my mind. No longer understanding anything at all of the inner chaos, in desperation, I turn to the Psalms. "They cry for help and Yahweh hears." But God remains deaf to my cry. Hour by hour I fight to stave off the descending darkness, and the rising cadence of the clickety-clack, clickety-clack running incessantly in my head.

As the day of Debby's debutantes' ball approaches, a deep dread takes hold of me. The night of the rehearsal, after Debby and I have supper, she goes off with her partner, and I follow in my Datsun.

Entering the vast hall, I immediately want to run away. Everyone is rushing about, and the cacophony of sound easily breaches my defences. I feel agitated, alienated, disorientated, restless. Clickety-clack, clickety-clack goes the train. The fire inside my head is stoked; the steam ready to blow. My body shudders, and my head is going to crack. I phone home. Elizabeth answers. "Please come and fetch me, Elizabeth!" I cry into the mouthpiece. "I'm too scared to drive myself. Come now. Now please!"

"George and I are leaving right away, Mom. Wait for us outside."

I find my way back to the main hall just as the girls make their entrance up to the stage. Debby waves her crimson ostrich feather. I want to scream and flee, but I force myself over to her and instantly begin to cry. "I'm going home with Elizabeth, Debs. Sorry I can't stay." The tension in my neck is unbearable. My brain is about to disintegrate. I battle to control myself as I make my way unsteadily outside.

The whole way home in the car George speaks about the effects drugs have on the limbic system. "It's the pills which are driving you crazy, Mrs. B. It's not you. You must stop the pills." Why can't I believe him?

By the time we reach home I am calmer. I tell Nicky what happened and he hushes me in his arms. "It's okay, Cookala. You're home now. I'll run you a bath, make you a cup of tea. A good night's sleep and you'll feel better in the morning." Clickety-clack. Clickety-clack. Jump in front. Jump in front and you won't come back.

My mind is grasping for something, anything to hold onto. I have a bath and swallow my cocktail. I never hear Nicky come to bed. I wake up in the very early hours of the morning bathed in sweat. In the bathroom I wash my face, then look in the mirror above the basin. The haunted face and desperate eyes that stare back at me are those of a stranger. Who is that person, I wonder? What have I become? I hang over the basin crying to myself, "I can't fight this anymore. How can I stop it? What can I do?

"Run away, Felicity. Change your name. Go to a foreign country. Drive the car and abandon it when it runs out of petrol. Become a tramp."

Options appear and then cancel themselves out one by one. I return down the passage, stop and stare into the bedrooms to study the innocent, vulnerable faces of my family peacefully asleep. How I love them. They deserve better than me.

My whole body begins shaking and again sweat pours off me—an alternative to my agony has suddenly crystallized. I can't bring myself to utter the foul word that tantalizes my tormented mind with a final, macabre solution: suicide. Self-loathing sweeps over me; I feel nauseous. How could I even think of killing myself? It's unthinkable! But I *am* thinking of killing myself. My head throbs; my vision blurs. A migraine is coming on.

In my confusion I leap at the problem of the migraine. I will get the headache under control and all will be fine by morning. Pills for the migraine and an ice-packed cloth for my cracking head, and all will be well. I return to bed, and not long after I hear the family preparing themselves for another day. Is it morning already?

I see them off, ice-pack pressed to my eye, saying nothing about the previous night's desperation. Telling myself I am back in control, I return to bed. But within minutes of their departure my anxiety returns more acute than before. I can't settle down in bed. I fidget, wring my hands, pace the passage. Clickety-clack. Clickety-clack goes the train. I look into the girls' bedrooms. Debby has laid everything out on her bed for the big night. Picking up the crimson ostrich feather, I know I won't possibly be able to attend the ceremony, and I burst into tears, sobbing, "I'm not going to be there tonight, Debs." Clickety-clack. Clickety-clack. I press my face into the white froth that is her dress, still sobbing, "I won't be here when you come back from school this afternoon!" Everything inside my cracking head is screaming, "You must be gone! You must be gone!" Clickety-clack. Clickety-clack. But where? How?

Holding my head to stop it from cracking, I walk to the kitchen saying to myself, "You must be crazy to think like this. You're her mother. Her mother." Uncontrollable tears. "You love her. Get hold of yourself!" Clickety-clack. Clickety-clack. "You must be gone! You must be gone!" My body trembles; my hands shake so much I can hardly fill the kettle to make myself a cup of tea. I open the drawer to take out a teaspoon . . . and there is Nicky's butcher knife.

Carrying both tea and knife, I return to bed, a mysterious measure of comfort washing over me. My frantic search is over. I don't have to run away. I can simply drop anchor here, now. The knife shows me, with searing clarity, where my solution lies.

But sudden fear intervenes, and, hysteria mounting, I see my Bible still lying open from the previous night's futile search for help. My Christian roots come to my rescue. I pick up the telephone before I can change my mind. Nicky answers, and I sob, scream, "Nicky, I can't go on anymore. I have your butcher's knife in my hand. Help me! I need you!" His reaction is calm and immediate. "Just stay where you are, Cookala, I'm on my way." Replacing the telephone on the cradle, I feel emotionally drained and physically exhausted. Tears stream down my face as I stare at the knife still in my hands.

Nicky, afraid he will not reach me in time, telephones a dear friend of mine who lives down the road. Within minutes she is with me. Moments later Nicky arrives with my mother and a priest in tow. They find the curtains still drawn and me still in my nightdress, knife in hand. My mother's serene presence calms the situation as she offers me tea and repeats several times to Nicky, "It's those damned pills." My face must tell them the whole story, for no one dares ask for the knife.

CHAPTER TWO

The Hour of Lead

It's as if a member of the family has died. Everyone is in a state of shock, and I'm not left alone for a minute. Nicky alternates between sitting next to me on the bed and frantically making phone calls to have me admitted to a city hospital with psychiatric facilities. Living outside the city limits, as well as being a private patient, makes this very difficult. In desperation, our family doctor steps in. He gives the hospital his sister's home address as my place of residence.

My daughters come home during the afternoon and find me still in bed. I feel a deep self-loathing as Nicky tells them I am not well and that he is taking me to the hospital for a few days. Cathy packs my weekend bag while I get dressed. When it is time to go, I lose whatever frail resolve I've been clinging to and plead that I be allowed to stay at home. But the priest, who has stayed the whole time, intervenes saying, "You need help, Felicity, you must go. You can't fight this anymore." I don't say goodbye to Elizabeth or Linda, or wish Debby well for her debutantes' ball. I'm too ashamed.

As we leave home darkness is falling, a portent of what is to come. Something indefinable inside of me has gone, been taken, lost. I feel cut off from Nicky, as well as Cathy, who has accompanied us. I'm floating outside time, adrift from myself, and it's a frightening sensation. I repeatedly ask them what is going to happen to me, and they continually reply, "Don't worry, we'll be with you all the time." As the kilometres fall rapidly behind us I become increasingly agitated.

"Please, Nicky," I beg, "turn back. I promise I'll do anything you say. Just take me home!" He pats my knee, reassuring me, "Don't cry, Fel. We're all in this together." Cathy leans over the back of my seat, "Don't worry, Mom. The doctor's going to tell us what's happening tonight. You won't be staying too long, I'm sure." I wring my hands in my lap and stare blindly out the window. The neon lights flashing their advertisements across the highway are meaningless images. But the wail of an overtaking ambulance siren awakens me from my stupor and makes my stomach knot, as it undoubtedly signals our proximity to the hospital.

It takes Nicky some time to locate the casualty entrance. Cathy is patting me gently on the shoulder as she directs him where to park. A cloak of darkness envelops me as Nicky opens the door and takes my shaking hand in his. Cathy links her arm through mine, and they ease me toward the ominously beckoning doors.

Stepping through the open doors is like coming upon a battlefield. Doctors dash from one cubicle to another, trying to tend to a seeming mass of patients. Stabbed people clutch at themselves, trying to staunch open wounds. Two drug addicts sit dazedly against a wall. Moaning people lie on chairs that have been pushed together, while paramedics unload road accident victims, still in shock, onto gurneys standing along the corridor. Orders are shouted from every direction. Even in my own disturbed state, I am acutely aware of the chaos before my eyes.

Nicky leaves me standing with Cathy while he goes off to admissions to complete the paperwork. My mind is chaotic. I want to drive an apple corer into my tingling scalp to let the pressure escape. I hang on tightly to Cathy's hand until Nicky returns with the papers, and then it is my turn to climb on the roundabout.

We walk down a long passage to a small room where I am asked to sit and wait for the doctor. He takes a long time in coming. Finally a flustered young man with red hair enters, sits down, glances at his watch and immediately asks, "What's your problem, Mrs. Bielovich?"

"I don't know, I don't know," I burst forth, sobbing uncontrollably. "Sometimes I want to drill a hole into my head to let the heat and racing thoughts out; other times I feel my head is cracking into pieces. I think I'm going crazy. My moods swing around like a weathervane. My ears buzz. I'm dizzy. My spatial perception has gone. I'm antisocial. I get so scared I want to run away from myself, hide from myself. And taking the pills doesn't make it go away." He fails to ask a single question about the pills I'm taking, simply nods in a way that reminds me he is pressed for time. "Sometimes all I want to do is die," I go on, "other times I feel like God." Now his interest is piqued.

"Have you ever been involved in anything satanic, Mrs. Bielovich? Have you ever felt like two people? Have you ever felt you were being persecuted? Do you hear voices?" I try to explain the clickety-clack of the train which throbbed out, "Jump in front, jump in front," inside my head.

"Tell me about this voice," he pursues. "Can you hear it? Does it talk to you? Do you talk back to it? How long have you been hearing it?" In a garbled way I tell him it's not an actual voice I hear; rather it's like the rhythmic beat of a drum or cave echo that demands to be heard.

"Is it perhaps a person who does the talking?" he carries on.

"No. I've told you it's not a person. It's a something I can't name. But I know it when it's going around inside my head."

Relentlessly he continues, "When did you hear this voice tell you to jump in front of the train the first time? Are you hearing it now?"

"Stop it! Stop it!" I scream, holding my sweaty palms to my temples. "There's no voice inside my head. It's cracked. Something slimy is being sucked out. I can feel it."

The questioning stops. He picks up the phone and says, "I'm sending Mrs. Bielovich up to you. She's very distraught. Just settle her in for the night." Where is he sending me? I wonder, and to whom?

As we walk hand-in-hand down the endless corridor, Nicky tries to reassure me, "Everything's going to be fine; I'm here with you."

Exiting the lift on the eighth floor, we find the doors to the psychiatric ward closed, a guard standing outside. He rings a bell and we are admitted. There is a murky glimmer of light coming from behind the nurses' station, where two nurses sit and read.

One stands and comes over to us. "You must be Mrs. Bielovich," she says, directing us to an office where she asks me several questions, including the apparent favourite, "Are you hearing voices?" What is this thing they have about hearing voices, I wonder. She straightens some papers on the desk and tells us to follow her. She leads Nicky and me to a room two doors away from the nurses' station, then abruptly turns to address my husband, "You may go now, Mr. Bielovich."

It's as if I've been doused with cold water. I need Nicky with me to see me settled in, to talk to me for a little while, reassure me. I panic, beg the nurse to let him remain just until I undress, but she flatly refuses. I begin to cry, pleading with her, and she becomes increasingly belligerent.

"Don't be so selfish, can't you see how tired and upset your husband is? Look at all the worry you have caused him. He has a long distance to travel. He has to leave now, and you must get to bed."

Even in my distraught state, I feel the burden of guilt placed on my shoulders. This is all my fault. Nicky is hesitant to leave, but the nurse ushers him towards the orange door we had entered. "Don't worry. We know what to do," she assures him.

When I see the door closing behind him, I rush down the corridor, screaming, "Nicky come back, don't leave me, don't leave me, I want to go home!" I bang repeatedly on the closed door with my fists. The sister pulls me away but, motivated by fear, I angrily push her away. She shouts to the other sister for assistance, calling the guard at the same time, and the three of them drag me back toward the assigned room.

Forgetting all about pain, my fused back and pelvis, I lash out with my arms and feet, kicking and punching. I scream, scratch, bite, struggling to free myself from their grasp. The three of them haul me, thrashing and gasping for air, onto the bed. The guard presses my shoulders down onto the pillow, while one sister lays across my legs. The other sister runs out of the room, returning within seconds, syringe in hand. When I see this, a new struggle erupts, as I fight to pull my dress down every time she lifts it. Finally they overpower me and I feel the vicious jab of the syringe penetrate my buttock. Mercifully, the bright horror fades to black.

I wake in the early hours of the morning to find myself in a bed with the sides up, like a child in a cot. I try to pull myself up but fall back in a stupor, the earlier events a confused blur. I waken again later, with a muzzy head and sore eyes, still in my clothes, and a nurse is standing at the foot of the bed. The only thing I notice about her is her oily face and equally oily hair plastered to her scalp. I am to get up, have a bath, go to breakfast and meet with the psychiatrist at 9:30. No explanations, no offer to familiarize me with the place. Just go, go, *go*.

I make my way down the corridor in search of the bathroom. When I find it, a haggard, bleary-eyed stranger stares back at me from the mirror above the basin. As I bend down to wash my face, a middle-aged man, his exposed paunch hanging over his pyjama cord, enters and stands alongside, scratching himself in the groin. He snorts and spits phlegm into the basin beside me, making me want to be sick. What is a man doing here in a women's ward? Another man comes in, unshaven, unkempt. He smells putrid. Then they all start shuffling in—men, women and young girls, like cockroaches from under the floorboards.

I stand aside and watch the women washing their faces, peering at themselves in the mirror, their heavy pouched eyes so much like mine. They make a pretence of making up their faces with a stripe of eye-shadow, a blur of lipstick applied to pursed lips, but no one really bothers with their hair. The young girls, wrists bandaged, their firm flesh quite unashamedly exposed, lift their legs into the basin to wash their feet. The air smells heavy with stale breath and flatulence. Manners, privacy, all are sluiced away as everyone jostles for position. Certain of them monopolize the inadequate facilities, obviously the veteran players on this sorry stage.

I soon realize I am not the only newcomer on the floor. There is also a very agitated young woman who wants everyone to know she was admitted during the night. With a degree of pride she adds that she is "bi-polar." Never having heard that term before, I follow the example of the others and ignore her.

The day staff come on duty as I leave the bathroom. I drift down the passage, bumping into a young nurse along the way. I apologize, and, turning to me, she says, "You must be Mrs. Bielovich." What told her I *must* be? My miserable face? A third eye? A stamp on my forehead? Then I realize that every detail of the previous night's behaviour must have been carefully communicated to her, and my reputation must already be set—*watch out, this lady bites!*

However, she turns out to be more civilized than the night nurse. She tells me where the dining room, TV room and psychiatrists' rooms are, and outlines the routine which I will have to follow. And with that I enter the dining room for breakfast.

To the left of me, like a mutant plant, are tendrils of green plastic chairs grouped in fours round small tables bolted to the floor, at which several people are already sitting. To the right are padded chairs encircling low wooden coffee tables cluttered with overfilled ashtrays and marked by white rim circles testifying to hot cups carelessly placed there. This obviously serves as the sitting room. Leading off both these areas are brightly painted orange doors, a stark reminder of the previous night's terror.

I sit down at an unoccupied table, and am immediately joined by two other patients. The younger of the two, an olive-skinned woman, introduces herself as Gail. "Why are you here?" she asks. When she learns that it is my first time inside a psychiatric ward, and that I don't know what is wrong with me or what to expect, she is eager to help. Having been here for six weeks, she is a fount of information. As each patient wanders into the dining room she jabbers on about them and their habits, labelling each of them in her own unique fashion. Not terribly interested, I can't help but note that it isn't hard to grasp the derivation of "Sucking Pig," "Toothpicker" and "Scratcher." Her voice suddenly turning serious, she confides, "Watch out for 'Fish-eagle,' the nurse in charge of the dining room. She has eyes in the back of her head and spies for the psychiatrists." She looks intently at me to see if I've understood. I grunt back at her.

A partitioned polystyrene box is thumped down in front of me on the table, startling me slightly. There is nothing remotely exciting inside, but brisk "trading" nevertheless commences immediately.

"I'll give you my toast for your orange," someone says.

"Three cigarettes for your box." Another voice.

Gail hasn't mentioned this aspect of the Institution's routine, and I'm so absorbed with the vigorous bargaining that I don't even hear the offer on my hard-boiled egg. I only realize one has been made when I see the egg disappearing from my box. Unperturbed, I sit and observe further transactions long enough to see that cigarettes are obviously the most valued commodity in this bizarre marketplace, followed closely by meat. It's also clear that trading bestows power, status.

After breakfast, it is time for the psychiatrist. My peculiar new life is only just beginning.

Walking into his small office I see a young, good-looking man, white shirt sleeves rolled up, sitting behind a desk. My mind is still numbed from the trauma and heavy sedation of the previous night, so the moment he asks how I am feeling the dam wall bursts, and I can't stop crying. He attempts to draw me out with questions, but disconnected images and events float only vaguely to the edge of my consciousness, and the minute I try to capture them they evade my grasp and drift into oblivion. The tired question, "Are you hearing voices?" is repeated over and over again. I wish I could say yes, because perhaps then I could start getting better.

Clearly feeling that he is making no headway, the young man soon leaves the room and returns a few minutes later with another psychiatrist, Dr. Paul. "We are not to be disturbed," says Dr. Paul to the nurse outside. He closes the door and stands directly in front of me. I look up to see a man of medium build, dressed in a charcoal-grey suit with a red tie, staring down at me through thick-lensed, horn-rimmed glasses. "Tell me *exactly* what is happening in your life, Mrs. Bielovich."

I take an instant dislike to him, but nevertheless describe my symptoms. He is quickly more interested in my past, relentlessly jabbing like an inquisitor into my childhood, adolescence and adulthood, trying to drag from me some confession of deep-set trauma. I cannot help him. I explain to him that, to the best of my knowledge, I had a happy childhood. "I was the fifth-born child," I stammer, "my brother Anthony was always my hero; my sister Margaret my playground defender. Rosemary was my confidante. I shared a bedroom with her all my life." I go on to explain that, with my parents, I was even more abundantly blessed. They led by example, established core values and lived by them. Dad was born in England, educated in Ireland, served as a Captain in the Indian Army, emigrated to South Africa and bought a cotton farm before he met my half-Irish mother. Aside from being a man of honour, humour and high principle he was also a religious man. At an early age, his stories captivated me, as did his tap-dancing and the ditties he loved to sing to my mother. With my mother we instinctively knew, as did she, that hers was the heart we turned to for support, advice, comfort. Her faith and belief in God's providence was profound.

None of this background satisfies Dr. Paul's unswerving probe. Finally he lays aside his inquisitorial role for a more conspiratorial one, "Would you like to tell me when you felt you were losing *it,*

Mrs. Bielovich? You can let *it* all out, you know. You don't have to hang onto any of *it* now you're here!"

Losing what? Hang onto what? I feel confused, not knowing how to satisfy his apparent need for the mysterious *it*. I try again to give an accurate account of what is happening inside me, but nothing significant becomes apparent, so he confers with his colleague and both agree a session with my husband is necessary. I am dismissed, and the nurse calls me over to sign out with all the others who are already forming a queue to attend "occupational therapy."

What a motley crowd of listless, morose-faced bodies we are, waiting, under the supervision of an aide, for the lift to arrive. As other people enter the lift on our journey down, I wonder if they can see we are psychiatric patients. Even if we don't look different, I certainly feel different. It strikes me that this is my first time in hospital as a vertical and not supine patient.

We are led into a vast well-lit room where the newcomers are directed by the therapists into a small side office. There we are asked questions about our hobbies and what we would like to do for the morning. The question of my hearing voices not being raised, I readily agree to take a tour of the room.

The first thing that catches my eye is a loom where a young woman is working with consummate skill. Alongside her, a woman is churning out metres and metres of curtains on an Elna sewing machine, as if her life depends on it. Walking around the room I see opened cupboards filled with unopened packets of wool, all colours of the rainbow. There is a similar variety of fabrics and embroidery silks waiting to be used. Under normal circumstances I would have been in my element, having this wealth of options at my disposal, but nothing appeals to me.

Continuing my tour, I watch "Bi-polar" being shown how to make a macrame pot-plant holder, while a young man next to her pulls wet cane from a big basin of water to begin working on a tray. He has just completed his first loop when an agitated, middle-aged lady with flaming red hair rushes over and snatches it. "This cane is for my basket," she hisses. A heated argument ensues. Suddenly the man grabs her wrist, trying to force her hand open. She bends down and bites his hand. He raises his hand to strike her but the therapist intervenes, castigating them for their behaviour. Neither apologizes. Both retreat sullenly to their section, looking for allies, but neither finds any. All of us are too engrossed in our own misery to care.

At the lower end of the room, narrow workbenches stand from corner to corner along the wall, at which several men are doing woodburning. I have never seen this before. I stand fascinated, staring over their shoulders. A paunchy man and his coarse counterpart are engaged in beltmaking, while a couple of women are turning out purses and key-rings with nimble fingers. I watch for a moment and then move on.

Still nothing appeals to me, and I finally return to the disappointed therapist. Idleness isn't on her agenda, so I am led off to a minuscule kitchen to the side of the office. "Why don't you make scones or a cake for morning tea," she suggests. All the ingredients are there and I grudgingly agree to make scones. I accidentally omit the baking powder, offering no apology for the "rocks" I place on the plate with an ochre crack down its middle. I am unaware that tea operates on a first-come, first-served basis, so when I return to the main room after cleaning up the kitchen, the milk jug is empty, as is the teapot, and brittle crumbs are all that remain of my miserable baking effort.

After tea we all gather in a circle on the floor. Large sheets of white paper and a handful of fat crayons are handed out. Everyone begins drawing but me. When this is completed we are asked to explain to the group what our illustration means to us. Seeing how articulate and in touch with themselves some of these patients are, and how easily this therapy accesses all sorts of personal information for the therapists, I'm glad I haven't drawn anything. I have nothing to offer or share with this group. My preference to not participate in the collective healing process is not well received by the therapists, but I couldn't care less.

At last "O.T." comes to an end and it is back along our earlier route via the orange doors. We sign in, lunches are traded, and we are given an hour to rest on the bed. For me this is a short taste of heaven, too soon interrupted by a call to "recreation." Once again we are back in the lift, this time descending to the very bowels of the hospital. We walk down snaking corridors, stopping outside the door of an unknown room while the therapist goes inside. She emerges with a net and ball. Down yet more corridors, with air-conduction pipes running just above our heads, finally emerging through a cavernous opening into the fresh air. The net is put into place, two teams line up and volleyball begins. With my spinal fusion, I have no intention of jumping about, so I'm given the task of fetching the ball whenever it rolls down the adjacent slope.

As the others play, I sit and watch the traffic and passers-by and wonder what I can possibly be doing playing volleyball at three in the afternoon. A helipad adjoins our makeshift volleyball court, and a chopper lands, unloading a strapped-in patient who is swathed in head bandages. I silently wish it was me wearing the bandages. At least then I would know what is wrong with me. What is wrong with me? What is wrong with me? I repeat the question to myself endlessly, but find no answer. I'm afraid there never will be an answer.

Once back on the floor, patients wander into the TV room, arguing over which channel to watch. They drape themselves over chairs, ashes dropping from their cigarettes in long pieces, waiting to be trod on by the next person sitting down. One gross man, dressed in a hospital dressing gown, approaches the sister for a cigarette and is told to return in two hours' time. Dejectedly he returns to his seat, offering the trade of a peach to a young woman, without success.

Nicky arrives that evening with extra clothes for me, and I burst into tears the moment I see him. "Please, Nicky," I beg, "take me home. I'm scared. I don't know what's going on. I don't like Dr. Paul, and I know one of the nurses doesn't like me."

"Don't worry, Cookala," he says, "I'll go and see what I can do."

Off he goes to see the nurse and psychiatrist, only to return with the news that I have to remain for a psychiatric profile. This leaves me in tears, and a sister arrives to show me to a four-bed ward, already occupied by two other patients.

I glumly unpack two dresses, a skirt, a blouse and pair of shoes into the locker next to the bed. Placing my nightgown under my pillow I realize again that I'm not in a ward for a sick body but for a sick mind. This confuses me. In this unknown territory I feel uneasy, filled with doubt. Just then the psychiatrist, Dr. Paul, whom I'd taken a dislike to that morning, ceremoniously enters the ward. He looks like a pompous stuffed peacock inflated with his own self-importance. He approaches the young woman lying on the bed opposite me, pulls the curtains round the bed, and says that he wants to examine her. The woman speaks quite clearly, very audibly. "Since when do I have to have an internal for something wrong with my head?" Ignoring her objection, he proceeds with the examination, then pulls back the curtains, and strides off down the ward. "You bloody little pervert, you screwball!" she yells after him.

I want to laugh. It strikes me as funny, her sitting on the bed, fists raised and clenched, letting out a stream of expletives. But then I think of him coming back to do the same thing to me, and I suddenly cringe. If he does I know I am going to kick him where it will hurt most. With this gloomy prospect before me, my first day at the hospital comes to a close, and my internship begins in earnest.

Within days I settle into the rigid routine of rising at 5:30 a.m., squaring up my bed, visiting the psychiatrist for a "mind session," then walking the endless sterile corridors to occupational therapy and "evaluations." Having arrived at the hospital without any of my medication, I now have no idea what is being prescribed, yet, three times a day, under the watchful eye of the sister or male nurse in charge, unknown drugs are administered. If I refuse, a probing finger is thrust into my mouth, marking me out as uncooperative; the penalty for which is having to step out of line and swallow them in front of everyone like a child.

Each morning we work out at a gym session under the fanatical supervision of David, a male nurse. He resembles a Greek god with his blond, curly hair and penetrating blue eyes, and he revels in the attention his well-muscled body receives from the young girls. Their familiarity with him amazes me. Because of my back, I am sometimes allowed to sit out, and I observe the various patients trying to keep up with his constant demand to go faster, *faster*. When I'm obliged to join in I repeat to myself, "Jump, jump, you crazy lump."

One morning, during our gym session, I am resting against the wall when a head pokes around the door requesting, "Mrs. Bielovich, please." I am more than happy to leave the room. Outside the door, a confident, finely featured, blue-eyed woman in her late thirties tells me to follow her. Walking behind her, I notice her black high-heeled patent leather pumps and silk stockings embracing well-turned ankles and coltish legs. She is wearing a knee-length polka dot suit, with a red silk scarf casually draped over her one shoulder. Her long, fine, silky hair falls in soft waves, midway between her shoulders. Everything about her is the antithesis of myself.

I am relieved when we finally arrive at her office tucked away in a remote corner, down another endless corridor. My relief soon dissipates, however, when I see all the paraphernalia waiting for me on her desk. Within five minutes of starting the various tests, under the pressure of a stopwatch, I am floundering. Having poor coordination and a mind that isn't at all sure where it is at the moment, I am failing the puzzles and block tests miserably. These are followed by pages and more pages of multiple-choice questions to answer with little ticks in boxes, much like an I.Q. test. Disconcertingly, many of these questions, once answered, reappear in another guise. Apparently she is trying to trap me in her search for that elusive something the psychiatrists are so earnestly digging for. I feel totally inadequate and intimidated throughout the process, and my low self-image disintegrates even further.

Leaving the office I bump into a young man on his way in for an evaluation. "This is my third time around; they won't give up till they dig up something," he says, winking at me ludicrously. This rattles me. I wonder how many sessions it will take for them to discover the mysterious *it* they are still after.

As the weeks go by I grow to hate the digging sessions with the psychiatrists. These are the men who literally determine who you are, and certainly what is going to happen to you. Having access to your deepest and most private thoughts, they have frightening power, and an insatiable hunger to know everything about your childhood, adolescence and adulthood. Probing, dissecting, searching, always wanting more, they look relentlessly for something sinister, juicy.

I am lucky. Of the two psychiatrists on our floor I am assigned to Dr. Nickel, the one with a heart. He at least gives the impression that he wants to help me as he embarks on his fruitless fishing trips. It seems that he is always trying to hook onto an event, a person, a situation to give him any clue to my troubles, but I don't have even a red herring to offer for his labours. If only I had a traumatic past to give him, I tell myself, my misery would be over. But I haven't been the victim of incest, child abuse, physical or emotional battering. Sibling differences yes, but all within the parameters of normalcy, as far as I know. There is simply no buried anger or hostility that I know of, and so we swim around in ever-diminishing circles.

I hate the mornings in hospital, even more than I did those at home, because here every downcast face in the ward mirrors my own wretched state of nothingness. Here I have no past, present or future; I am simply taking up space in the sick air. And it is sick. I am accustomed to being in wards where people speak to each other about their husbands, children, family; where operations are compared. I've always been able to swap a magazine, share a chocolate or a cold drink with a fellow patient, to enjoy the flowers and cards sent by people out there who are rooting for our recovery. But here, in this wasteland, there is nothing to say. Here we have no lives outside our self-centred sickness. We are as sterile as the ward. I am shutting down. I can feel it.

Yet I am not unaware of the peripheral events happening around me. Whenever there is a commotion on the floor, or the arrival of a hysterical patient, my ears prick up, and I glance surreptitiously into the room where the sounds are coming from. The high turnover of young girls admitted with bandaged wrists makes a deep impression on me, as do the pasty, pale-faced ones who are off-loaded unceremoniously onto their beds after a stomach pump. Then there are the crying, anguished parents, following in the wake of their damaged children, muttering and blaming themselves, "If only we had listened to her, if only we'd spoken about it earlier." But when the doctor or nurse emerges, their defences are instantly up, and they carry on about how they've always done their best, given her everything, done everything.

If only they could join us in O.T. There in the privacy of our confessions, they would easily discover what the problem was. Even in my miserable state it is easy to see how many of these young girls are simply craving love, support and understanding from their parents, not possessions. They feel discarded, neglected, in the way. For some, having an attentive, listening audience for the first time in their lives causes them to overdramatize and embellish their stories, but being allowed to give vent to their feelings certainly appears to make a difference. One girl tells us she has attempted suicide five times to gain the attention she so desperately desires from her parents.

So our little community of pill-poppers, wrist-slashers, psychotics, neurotics and schizophrenics comes together daily to feed upon our emotional instability. I soon realize from the confessions that many are obviously victims of family, friends or social circumstances, and so I envy them. They have a clear reason for being here, and someone to blame. They should be thankful. All they have to do is state the facts, change their attitude, communicate, move on. For me, it isn't that simple. I drift among the flotsam and jetsam of the foundering ship that is my mind, from one unanswered question to another, never knowing the cause of my own particular fall overboard. Gradually, I arrive at a firm conclusion—there must be something pathologically wrong with me which no one will tell me about.

I speak to one of the O.T. therapists about this, and she says it is common for depressed people to feel this way because they can't *see* what is wrong. She tries to reassure me that turnover of psychiatric patients in O.T. is brisk. No one stays for long. I want to believe her; I hope she is right, but trying to read a book that afternoon doesn't make me feel very reassured. No matter how hard I try to concentrate I can't connect with the story. I give up trying, turning instead to the creation of a linen cross-stitch tablecloth. The Croatian priest visits and sees me sitting in the dining room, monotonously poking the needle in and out, and he despairingly says, "Get out of yourself; put it away. Talk to people. Play table tennis. Do something. Don't just sit there. If you want to get better *do* something." Like what? I think to myself. The only thing I want to do is punch his face.

With endless patience the therapists try to interest me in croquet or table tennis, but they never succeed in getting me to participate in any group activity because I have my spinal fusion as an excuse. Not even when they take the trouble to organize a really good picnic lunch outside do I join in. I don't want any part of any of these people. I don't want anything.

One afternoon, while appearing busy at the loom, I see an elderly woman undressing just outside the therapist's office. I simply sit and watch her, as if I'm at the movies. One article after another is removed, and she is almost naked when a balding man in his late sixties enters the room, takes off his jacket, covers her and leads her away. I find out later through the grapevine that she has been admitted for Alzheimer tests. The incident disturbs me. Why hadn't I helped her?

Nicky visits me every night, while during the day three of our daughters come between lectures. They often find me busy knitting a multi-coloured scarf, already several metres long, but no one ever asks when it is coming to an end. They praise my macrame and basket-making efforts, applaud my amateur pottery bowl, believing these are signs of progress. The psychiatrist knows otherwise. He sees I am merely ticking over, operating on automatic pilot.

My husband and daughters are interviewed extensively by Dr. Nickel, without success. No new light is shed by way of previous abnormal behaviour, and so he tries another approach. He hands me over to Professor Mindle, Head of Psychiatry. I have seen other patients called from O.T. to see the professor in Room 26. They often return in tears, and I've wondered why. Now it's my turn to find out.

Room 26 means another journey down endless rabbit warren hallways, this time with a cantankerous woman urging me to walk faster, faster. "Can't keep the professor waiting." I arrive before a green door, out of breath and scared. Knocking on the door while in the process of opening it, she curtly announces, "Mrs. Bielovich, Professor."

"Come in and sit down, Mrs. Bielovich," he says authoritatively, patting a plastic chair near to him. Nervously I sit down. Seated in a semi-circle facing me are eleven eager-looking students with notebooks on their laps. Dr. Mindle opens the interview with a matter-of-fact, "Today I am presenting forty-three-year-old Mrs. Bielovich. She is a first-time patient in a psychiatric ward. She was actively psychotic on arrival." He then gives them a brief synopsis of what is in my psychiatrist's report, and asks the students if they have any questions they would like to put to me. I can't believe it. It is open season. I feel like some rare artefact as they turn me round, inside-out and upside-down, never once using my name when asking a question.

The spotlight soon comes to rest on my moods and behaviour. One student arrives at the conclusion that my being the fifth child may have something to do with my poor self-image. Perhaps, she suggests to the professor, my parents hadn't wanted me. Maybe it is a simple case of rejection. Like divers in search of oysters, they probe into my subconscious hoping to find the pearl which will give them their answer. But all they do is disturb troubled waters and increase the doubt in my mind as to my own sanity. At no time do they question my medication, of which they must be aware via my report. In the end it feels like finding the answer isn't the goal for these earnest pupils; the goal is rather to impress the professor by offering penetrating insights into the *object* under analysis. I am being used so everyone can display their brilliance.

The interview over, I am peremptorily dismissed, nervously trying to digest all their analyses. I feel degraded, diminished, dehumanized by the whole experience, and not being told about their learned findings, I'm only further confused about my own mental capacity.

As the weeks turn toward months, both Nicky and I know that I'm not making any progress. In fact I am worse. Whereas at home I had been trying to cope, fighting for survival, here I have completely given up. My well-groomed appearance is a thing of the past, and I have become a formless, purposeless lump of dough.

I have been in the hospital for over two months now. The corridors no longer frighten me. I have earned the trust of the occupational therapists, who allow me to go to the toilet outside the room unattended. Familiar as I am with my surroundings, however, the one thing I can't get used to are the lifts. I still resent the healthy people entering "our" lift carrying flowers and gifts for someone *sick* they are visiting. Because we have no external signs of illness we appear normal to them. Maybe if we wore straitjackets, foamed at the mouth, shrieked obscenities, they would realize we are also sick. I resent them further because they're unaware we have lost our most prized possession—our freedom. When their visiting hour is up they can choose whatever they want to do, go wherever they want to go. They are masters of their universe, while we are slaves to routine, tablets and authority.

Several days after my degrading session with the professor and his students, Dr. Nickel calls me back in for a chat. He tells me I'm not making any progress—as if I didn't know that. He wants to discuss electro-convulsive therapy—shock treatment—with my husband tonight. I put up no resistance, simply cry the entire time. I never ask how long it will take, whether it will hurt, or cure me. It no longer matters. This lump of dough is theirs. Since I no longer own myself, there is no sense resisting the procedure. My husband's consent is all that's necessary.

Squaring up my bed that morning of my first treatment, I still don't care what happens to me. I have breakfast, attend gym as usual, during which I am called away by the sister-in-charge. Without speaking to me, she leads me down a short corridor, through orange doors into the ECT room. It is very small. The doctor's examination couch stands in the centre, reminding me of an operating table, as does the fluorescent light above it. I'm nervous. My legs are leaden. The paraphernalia laid out neatly on the trolley in the corner does little to allay my fear. Without explaining the procedure to me, the nurse asks me to lie down and wait for the doctor. My heart is pounding. My tongue feels thick, my eyes bulbous. Dr. Nickel confidently enters the room, but he too fails to explain the procedure. "It's not going to hurt," is all he says as he comes to stand behind me. The sister hands him what appear to me to be two round discs. She wraps a blood-pressure band around my arm, gives me an injection "to relax," places a gag in my mouth and a mask over my face. "Breathe deeply," she orders. The rubbery smell of the snorkel-like mask as it's placed over my nose is something I will never forget.

I don't feel a thing physically. But mentally I do. I feel emotionally scarred, forever stigmatized, as if the fact of the shock treatment is somehow emblazoned across my face. Otherwise I feel no different than before. I enter the deserted ward and am overwhelmed by a feeling of terrible loneliness, struck again by the total absence of flowers. I'm offered a cup of tea and told to report for O.T. after an hour's bed rest. A young Salvation Army girl who received shock treatment directly after me also returns to the ward, eyes staring into space, a mirror-image of myself, and I remember Jack Nicholson's character in *One Flew Over the Cuckoo's Nest*. I am certain I too will end up lobotomized.

I never voice these fears, giving them power to fester and breed like fungi in the dark recesses of my mind. Later they will resurrect and haunt me. Feeling tainted, resentful and angry with myself for having lost control of my brain for those few moments, I won't admit to anyone that I've undergone ECT.

Eight more treatments follow. Eight more times I am escorted down the corridor, through the orange doors and into the small room with its harsh fluorescent light and morbid tray of sterile equipment. Still I feel no different, and so my final disintegration becomes inevitable. A new kind of despair settles on me. I am going to remain enmeshed in myself forever. There is no escape. Throughout my life, whatever the circumstances, I have clung to my faith and been sustained by it, but now a seeping despair sucks at its solid foundation, and my faith begins to crumble. I don't analyse it; I only know that, despite all, I will never let go of my God. If I am going to be erased like the characters on a computer, or go down into Hades, then He is coming with me. We will be entombed together, reduced, silenced, dormant together.

Various members of the family visit on Sunday afternoons, but I withdraw into my shell, completely alienating myself from them. No longer knowing where I belong or who I really am, I feel like a cup without a handle. When the girls enthusiastically tell me all they are doing I want to scream. Doing is a word which has disappeared from my life.

When Cathy tells me she has arranged a day pass with the psychiatrist for me to attend her graduation, I refuse to go. The loathing I have for the *thing* I have become is simply too deep. But she insists, arriving on the day not only with a new outfit for me, but also curling tongs, stockings and make-up. Ignoring my pleas to leave me where I am, she hustles and bustles me into my clothes. "Come on, Mom. It won't be the same without you. I want you there. So does

Daddy. He's waiting for us in the car." She is close to tears when she adds, "Please try to make this a happy day for us."

I see Nicky looking so proud and happy alongside the car, and it makes me feel worse. My anxiety is heightened when I see all the parents, students and Cathy's friends standing outside the great hall of the university, excitedly talking to each other. I want to run away. I'm a misfit here. I don't want to be part of any celebration. But Cathy pushes me forward, insisting that I have a family photograph taken. As it's taken no amount of coercion can draw a smile from my frozen face.

During my tenth week in O.T., having mastered nearly all the hobbies, I wander aimlessly down to the tool bench one morning and sit down next to the obvious outsider in the group. He'd come in a couple of days before and rumour has it he is an ex-convict. The therapists have said not to fraternize with him but, being anti-establishment, anti-everything in fact, I befriend him not only out of curiosity, but because I also consider myself an outsider.

I initiate our first conversation. "Teach me woodburning," I blurt out, something between an order and a plea. But, apparently feeling neither threatened nor superior, he agrees, instructing me with great skill, and an immediate affinity springs up between us, rooted in our perceived worthlessness. His name is Jack and he has grown up fighting for survival. He is in his late twenties, lean of body, with dark brown, penetrating eyes. He's gently spoken, with strong bony hands constantly fidgeting in and out of his pockets, like a squirrel foraging for nuts. Jack always wears tatty, faded blue jeans, and likes to impress upon me that his tapered shoes are genuine leather. They certainly look it, and he takes great pride in keeping them spit and polish clean.

He shares a whole new world with me. His language, descriptive and coarse, never offends as we share our most intimate thoughts and feelings in total honesty. Many times he mirrors exactly what I am feeling. Status and backgrounds are irrelevant; we don't probe, dig, ask questions. We simply compare and explore our feelings, and in doing so layer upon layer of self-revelation pours out. We trust each other implicitly. Feeling so safe and utterly transparent with each other, our real selves, in all their weaknesses and strengths, surface in a climate of mutual, nonjudgmental acceptance. The fact that he was jailed for housebreaking and being in possession of dagga* never worries me at all.

When I am with him, an air of normalcy pervades, extending into the dining room where we casually eat out of each other's boxes, as well as into the corridor where we often share a hot-chocolate nightcap together.

During our chats I discover his emotionally impoverished background and *raison d'être* for his prison sentence, pending the outcome of his psychiatric profile. Comparing notes on our experiences under the evaluator's stop-watch, we laugh at how stupid we appeared on the outside, when we know we are so clever on the inside! Mimicking the psychiatrist, which Jack is really good at, is his favourite pastime, and it works to take the sting out of the many negative things we have been told about ourselves.

We must appear an odd couple to the staff and various onlookers, but the more we share our experiences, *sotto voce*, the more relaxed and trusting we become. Then comes the afternoon that is to change the course of my life. My feet are too swollen to go outside for croquet and Jack has been told to stay behind for another assessment. In the interim we make our way to the TV room. For the first time we are unattended, entirely alone. We both feel the silence and intimacy, but sit down next to each other without awkwardness of any kind. We gossip about the punch drunk former boxer who shares his ward, bragging endlessly about his glory days, and about the retired "general" who is actually a jobless ticket-puncher.

Unabashed, I tell him about the antics of the woman in my ward who wears harlot underwear. He laughs, admitting that he is turned on by all the exposed flesh he sees in the ablution centre every

* marijuana

morning, that he longs for a "dolly" in his arms, even a pill-popping one. He asks me what it is like being married to the same man for so long. Do I want or need a man? Strangely, I never feel his questions invade my privacy. He is so sensitive, such a good listener. His reasoning is uncomplicated, direct. Hastily, we empty the well of our feelings, draining our self-centred doubts and fears in huge drafts, both scared we may be interrupted before excising our greatest fear. Are we indeed crazies?

Jack senses I believe this to be true in my case, but he won't hear of it. "If they knew what was wrong with you, my friend, they would tell your husband, not keep you here like a resident," he assures me. "I'm telling you, they're still fishing. Listening to you speak, you sound just like me a few years ago when I was popping all sorts of pills every day. Back then, I thought that I was crazy too. But it's not you that's crazy. It's the pills that make you crazy. If you want the craziness to stop, quit the pills."

I start to cry. "How can I quit when the nurse watches me like a hawk all the time?"

He puts his arm around my shoulder reassuringly, "You don't have to stand in the queue anymore if you don't want to . . . just run away."

"Run away where?" I ask, taken aback.

"Anywhere nearby, so they can still find you."

"What will happen to me when they do?"

"That's the good part. They'll transfer you to another place, a state psychiatric institution. I've been to one before. You don't have to worry about pills there, because they don't give any."

Jack has me convinced. My emotional ground is so fertile, that the seed doesn't even need time to germinate. I decide to go that very evening when the staff hand over. I say nothing to Jack over supper. Instead I gave him my plate, telling him I'm not feeling very well. I leave the dining room without saying goodbye to him, my mind occupied with how to slip past the guard without being seen.

Back in my ward I fidget, anxious for hand-over time to arrive.

Hysterical screams are coming from a young girl, a new arrival in the ward next door. The usual hurried footsteps, the clang of the sides of the bed as they are pulled up, the screams suddenly silenced, all this disturbs and frightens me. As of tomorrow she belongs to *them,* and they'll begin to scrutinize her impenetrable darkness, searching for an explanation, an illness, a label. Soon deathly silence draws me out of my ward, and I see a supine, corpselike young girl with heavily bandaged wrists. But I don't linger.

I make my way cautiously past the open door of the psychiatrist's office. The blurred voices of the girl's parents reassure me that he will be occupied for a while. There is a hive of activity as I nervously approach the nurses' station. Can they hear my heart beating, my mind turning itself inside out? Will they notice my furtive, darting eyes? I must be cool, relaxed, calm. The nurse who'd jabbed me in the buttock on my arrival is immersed in conversation, strengthening my resolve. I slip past, holding my breath.

Now I must get past the guard standing outside the door. Ignoring the turmoil in my mind I approach him, saying impassively, "I have permission to go to the chapel and will be back in twenty minutes." He looks me up and down, then lets me go without any fuss.

I breathe a sigh of relief and walk down the corridor. Another night nurse comes into view. Like an escaped prisoner all I want to do is run, run, run. She asks me where I am going. Surely she can see my fear, my feverish cheeks. I suck in my frayed nerves and calmly give her the same story. Having no purse, or anything else in my hands, she believes me, waving me on. I wave back, my heart pounding like a jackhammer.

Alighting from the lift, I turn right into the flow of arriving visitors. Just as they have never recognized my psychiatric status, my walk to freedom also goes unnoticed. A stickler for the truth, I stop briefly at the chapel before making a resolute departure towards the welcoming open doors of the main hospital entrance. Without thought of consequence I step out into the falling dusk.

Now outside the hospital, I have no idea whatsoever where to go. I have no money, and I'm dressed in winter clothes in the middle of summer, as the air-conditioner in the hospital is always so brutally efficient. The first place that comes to mind, because of its proximity, is an isolated park, notorious for its violent incidents.

Walking along the pathway toward the park, I watch the passing traffic, marvelling at the commuters going home, to the theatre, somewhere. I plod on until I arrive at the locked entrance of the park. Undaunted, I climb over the fence and work my way up along the winding path toward the highest ground of the park.

I'm normally scared of the dark, but this night holds no terrors for me. Godlike, invincible, I stagger through the black mosaic until I come upon my throne, a large, flat rock. I sit, and from where I sit I can see the windows of my ward in the hospital. But they can't see me. Some mysterious, hidden power has not only protected me but also made me invisible! Then I see a shooting star cut across the inky skies and I'm sure I have inspired it. It never occurs to me that Nicky will not find me when he arrives to visit, and that chaos will ensue.

Sitting there quietly, I do no thinking, but as time ticks by I am grateful for my knitted dress as it cools down. After several hours of welcome solitude, I hear my name being called over and over again by my husband, brothers-in-law, and a posse of policemen. Momentarily panic-stricken, I hide in a bush, watching their torches flashing up the steep pathway towards me. Various men peer and poke into the dense shrubbery. I hold my breath as someone passes directly by me, then the shrub behind me is suddenly pushed aside and I am face to face with my husband. I don't know who is more surprised.

Nicky is quickly joined by the others of the search party, and emotions run high. Comments fly about how irresponsible my behaviour is, how ashamed I should be for the anxiety I have caused. Nevertheless, within this clamour of condemnation, my husband's reaction is extraordinarily kind and nonjudgmental; he is simply relieved at finding me unharmed.

The taste of freedom I've had has strengthened my spirit in some strange way, because driving back to the hospital I don't feel scared about my decision or its outcome. However, when I step out of the lift back into confinement, a barrage of recriminations begins.

"Where the hell have you been?" screeches the nurse who originally admitted me, grabbing me tightly by the arm, shaking me like some rag doll, "Do you know all the trouble you have caused everyone with your stupidity? Just wait till the professor hears about this!" She marches me into his consulting room. "He'll sort you out once and for all," she adds harshly as she dials his home number. I hear the phone ringing and then being answered. "Sorry to wake you up at one o'clock in the morning, Professor, but Mrs. Bielovich ran away this evening, and we have just had her returned to us by the police. What would you like us to do with her?" I can't hear his reply, but she smiles smugly as she replaces the phone on the cradle. "He's very, very angry, Mrs. Bielovich. He doesn't like being woken up at the best of times. He's on his way over right now to deal with you in person."

"Let him come," I think to myself. With Nicky at my side, rubbing my cold hands the whole time, I don't feel the least scared or intimidated.

The nurses jump to attention the moment they hear Dr. Mindle's footsteps enter the psychiatric ward. I hear them prattle out their answers before his questions are even asked, "We would have phoned you earlier, Professor, but we didn't want to alarm you. I believed her when she told me she was going to the chapel to pray. We searched the hospital the minute we found her missing. Her husband called the police. We phoned you the moment she was found."

Entering the room, Dr. Mindle looks most unprofessorlike, with his pepper-corned chin and creased open-neck shirt, and he shows no concern whatsoever for my well-being as he goes straight to what he considers the relevant point, "Do you know what you did here tonight, Mrs. Bielovich, by pulling a stunt like this?" Before I can answer he rants on, "I'll tell you what you did. You put this hospital's reputation at risk; you showed no regard for the nurses who have cared and looked after you these past three months, and you've managed to upset all the other patients who had to be questioned as to your whereabouts." The nurses all nod their heads in agreement. He nods back, "If it hadn't been for the sharp eyes of one of the nurses seeing you chatting to Jack this afternoon, nobody would have had any idea where you could possibly be. As it is, only a wild guess on his part suggested the park nearby."

The nurse I dislike gives me a smug, condescending smile as the diatribe continues, "I can't and won't have irresponsible behaviour like yours on my floor." He turns to Nicky, "You must try and understand my position, Mr. Bielovich. I have all the other patients to consider. I can't have patients simply doing whatever they like. I don't have any other alternative than to transfer your wife to another place." The professor stares at me long and hard, as if waiting for me to speak. Nicky just stands, rubbing his chin and shaking his head. I keep quiet. The professor rises, leans over his desk and rifles through various papers. "Nurse Saunders, have you seen the papers for certifying patients?" She hasn't. "Don't worry," he says, "I'll phone Dr. Heslop and the magistrate and speak to them directly." His steely grey eyes pierce into mine as he dials their numbers and informs them, "I'm so sorry to wake you up at this ungodly hour, but I'll be needing your signature first thing in the morning to commit a troublesome patient of mine to a state psychiatric institution."

He puts down the telephone, with a look of satisfaction on his face and says, "Mrs. Bielovich, the papers certifying and committing you to a state facility will be ready for your husband to collect from the magistrate before nine o'clock this morning. I'm going home now and I hope you'll apologize to the nurses for the trouble you've caused, and give them no more. Good night. I'll see you before you go in the morning."

The drama over, I am told to say good night to Nicky, and, desperate as I am to have him stay and hear my side of the story, I remain calm and say good night to him in front of everyone. Leaving the office, I see Jack standing in pyjamas in the corridor. Our eyes meet. "Jeez, you got me into big trouble," he says. I apologize, but fail to thank him for what I hope will be sound advice.

The male nurse who leads me back to my room returns ten minutes later with a cup of hot chocolate and some biscuits. "Things could have been worse," he comments. I ask him what he means. He says that having easy access to them, he is on drugs himself and understands. He makes me smile when he adds that he takes tablets to prevent himself from joining the crazy people on the floor.

Next morning, the moment lights come on at 5:30 David brings me a cup of tea and tells me that where I am going things will be very different. He doesn't have time to elaborate, because the night nurse comes in and tells me to strip my bed, pack my bag and get ready to leave with the police. She is still smarting from the night before, and I can sense her satisfaction in ordering me around.

Breakfast is like being in Coventry. No one is allowed to even approach me. But then, as I stand up to leave, I'm met with an array of thumbs-up signs from the patients, and I realize we have become a little community, and I am touched.

At 9 a.m. promptly, Dr. Mindle summons me to his office where Nicky and my daughter Cathy are already waiting for me. They are visibly shaken by the turn of events. The professor opens my file, checks that all is in order, and reiterates that my behaviour has forced him to commit me to a mental institution. Taking into account that my husband is a police reservist, he magnanimously allows Nicky to escort me there, provided I guarantee that I will cause him no further trouble.

Stepping through the hospital doors again, this time into the light of day, I am elated to be leaving Dr. Mindle and his hostile minions. But I feel like an expelled pupil too. Punishment is in order, and as we walk toward the car, the harsh words spoken by Dr. Mindle echo in my mind . . . "committed" . . . "mental institution." How can this possibly be happening to me?

CHAPTER THREE

The Judas Window

The sixty-kilometre drive to the Institution is a sombre journey. The full impact and implication of my being certified and committed to a mental institution continues to sink in for me. "Certified and committed to a mental hospital." The words repeat themselves over and over as I try to make sense of my situation. What must Nicky and Cathy be feeling? I don't ask them. I'm too preoccupied with my own concerns.

Upon arrival we are greeted by two forbidding gates opening to a long, desolate and twisting driveway which leads us to a set of enormous, old red-brick buildings. Unlike the city hospital, here there is no hustle or activity to be seen. In fact, aside from a few people walking around in small groups, it reminds me of a vacant school, a notion which I find distinctly disturbing.

My stomach twists as Nicky parks the car under the shadow of some splendid blue-gum trees, and quietly announces we have arrived. A young woman dressed in a grey uniform approaches us and addresses Nicky, "Glad to see you didn't get lost on the way, Mr. Bielovich. You certainly made it in good time."

"Hello, Mrs. Bielovich," she says, turning to me with a smile on her face. "Professor Stack is expecting you. If both of you follow me, I'll take you to his office. Your daughter can bring your bag inside and help you unpack it afterwards." Her calm friendliness assures me somewhat, and I allow myself to think at least briefly that this place will be better for me.

We enter Professor Stack's office and I recognize my bulging file lying on his desk. I immediately feel uneasy, wondering what horrid things are contained in there about me. To my relief, he appears disinterested in the file and simply places his hand on it as he begins questioning me.

The drabness of his office is in sharp contrast to the clinical whiteness and the correctness I have left behind at the city hospital. Under normal circumstances, the pressed ceilings would interest me, but I focus instead on the faded floral curtains standing sentry in the wood-framed window, through which a whisper of a breeze tries to enter. The walls are bare. No testimonials. No posters. An old, unpolished teak desk stands on the bare wooden floor, and tatty medical books, their broken spines piteously propping each other up, seem to confirm my uneasiness. Certainly this must be the last outpost for the broken and discarded members of society. People like me, I think to myself.

Professor Stack is a thick-set, intelligent-looking man in his late sixties with large brown eyes. "Right, Mrs. Bielovich," he says kindly, leaning back in an old-fashioned office chair, "let's try and get to the bottom of this. I want you to feel absolutely free to say whatever you like about yourself, your family, friends, anything that comes to mind. Don't be frightened. There are no tests, time limits or anything we have to prove to each other."

I'm so overwhelmed at being treated as a normal person that I become very emotional. "I don't know if I am crazy, but nothing makes sense to me anymore," I cry. "I live in a nightmare, where everything—time, people, places, things—are pulled into each other as if by some magnetic force over which I have no control. I'm so tightly locked into it, I can't escape, and I'm terrified I may never get out of the nightmare."

He remains silent for a moment before speaking. "Try not to worry about the future," Mrs. Bielovich, he says compassionately. "Perhaps, if you could tell me why you ran away from the hospital last night, we can work our way back to where you felt everything started getting confused."

It all comes out in a torrent, garbled and confused, but he listens with apparent empathy, never interrupting. At the end of my narrative I feel he's probably got the most accurate, coherent picture of me as a person that any doctor has gained in all my time in hospital. Finally, he says to me, "I certainly don't see you spending the rest of your life here. I'm confident that with time and little or no medication you will recover and lead a normal life." This is the first grain of hope I've been given, and I weep with relief.

My meeting over, the sister leads us to the ten-bed ground floor dormitory. She mentions rather ominously that the upper floor is strictly out of bounds. As we enter the dormitory, I look around and it's clear that the professor's drab office was splendid by comparison. Directly in front of me is an alcove where two small iron beds stand, separated only by the width of a narrow window partially covered by indistinguishable threads serving as curtains. Resting against the foot of the bed is an upholstered chair with obscene lumps of kapok poking out of the seat. The armrests, with their little cocktail side-rests, have the familiar white rings from years of abuse, as does a three-legged teak table. The fourth leg, resting on the brown linoleum floor, is made up of tatty, outdated magazines. Alongside the table are two very old ladder-back chairs, their once leather-padded seats now sunken wells.

To the left of the doorway are three other beds, to the right five. In front of these five beds are three separate closed rooms with letterboxlike openings near the top of solid doors—spy holes, like in a prison cell. I stare at these tiny windows, and the name Judas springs to mind. I don't know why.

My bed is the last one in the left corner. In the opposite corner stands an old oak dressing-table, with only its cracked centre panel bearing testimony that it had been grand in its heyday. Between the beds, with nary a centimetre to spare, are chipped enamel lockers. These hold no water jugs or glasses, and mine is held closed by a wad of paper. There are no curtains around the beds to provide the relative privacy I had known at the hospital.

"This place is awful," I say looking around.

Cathy nods with tear-filled eyes. There is no reproach, only concern in her voice when she says, "But this is where you wanted to come, remember?"

"I know," I say, "but I didn't expect this. Never mind, I'll get by. I won't be here for long. I'll soon be home." The truth is that I feel the dormitory is exactly what I deserve, and when Nicky, always concerned about my back, requests a bedboard, I turn it down believing I deserve to sleep on the lumpy coir one provided.

This time there are no hysterics from me when Nicky and Cathy say goodbye. I wave back at them quite cheerfully as they peer out of the car window and return down the long drive. I can't understand why Cathy is crying.

Once they are out of sight, I return to the dormitory searching for the bathroom. To do this, I have to pass the three closed letter-box doors. The area is deserted and curiosity gets the better of me. Nervously, I lift the shutter to take a little peep. The room appears bare. I poke my nose further into the opening, and there, in the corner, I see a young woman lying on a mattress, curled up in a foetal position. She hears me raise the shutter, or perhaps it's my sudden intake of breath, and she screams violent obscenities at me. I drop the shutter as if I've been scalded, and, feeling frightened, hurry off.

Entering the ablution block, I realize this is going to be a day of comparisons with the hospital. There are two short, narrow toilet cubicles, both latchless. One doesn't have toilet paper on the wire triangle stapled to the cracked wall; the other has a questionable pool of water on the floor. I enter the one with the toilet paper, and abruptly must defend my territorial rights. There is a shove at the door, and I'm obliged to stretch out my leg to avoid being invaded. As I emerge, I am pushed aside by a young girl who rushes in, grabs the roll of toilet paper, and disappears down an unknown passage with it.

The two cracked, dirty-rimmed porcelain hand basins, poxed with carelessly left cigarette butts, have taps which refuse to respond to any twist or turn. Their continual drip explains the ugly rust stains. There isn't any liquid or cake soap as at the hospital either; only a sour, damp-smelling circular towel hanging on a tired brass rod.

The sound of a bell summons me to the dining room for lunch. As I cross the hall, women come in from outside and others push their way down the stairs. Falling in behind them, I suddenly realize that I am a prisoner in a new cage. The room looks like a small school hall. All the chairs stand against the wall, an ancient piano in one corner, and several tables are bunched up in another. The women pull these away and place four chairs at each of the tables, seven in all, each covered with a gaudy plastic tablecloth of either orange, green or brown. They promptly begin laying the tables with thick glasses, steel cutlery, eight slices of bread, a saucer of jam, several slices of butter, and a jug of water. I remain in the doorway until a nurse emerges from the opposite doorway. "Bielovich, find a chair and sit!" she barks.

There is sullen silence as I sit down at a table in the centre of the room. Grace is followed by a sudden mass exodus towards a push-and-shove queue. Not knowing the system, I am last in line. Although I can't see the food trolley, I certainly hear it as it squeaks and rumbles toward the yapping queue. By the time it is my turn to be served, there is only one mingy, meatless mutton bone floating in a watery liquid containing several peas, slivers of carrots and a piece of potato which had somehow avoided the scoop of the prehistoric ladle. Returning to the table I find one slice of bread. There is no conversation. I eat in dumb silence.

Lunch is followed by a holy hour on the bed, only mine isn't particularly holy. The bed is too narrow, my feet touch its bottom, and the mattress is uncompromisingly uncomfortable. I now wish that I had accepted Nicky's request of a board. But I don't complain. It's part of the punishment I deserve.

After my "rest," the nurse accompanies me on a walk round the grounds, explaining the rules, routine and roster, emphasizing that I am never to walk anywhere alone.

At afternoon tea, I see that each little job is done by one of us. Someone fills the urn, another puts out the cups and saucers, while yet another measures out the tea leaves, makes the tea and leaves it to stand. Determined not to miss out as I had at lunchtime, I hurry to help myself. Like everything else, however, tea leaves have been rationed. When I pour my tea, there are no leaves left in the pot, all having obviously passed through the hole in the strainer. I decide to forgo tea.

Recreational therapy has us confined in a small dark room where the lumpy couches, worn chairs, closed windows and oppressive humidity revolt me. As does a lanky woman with cracked, high-heeled patent leather shoes who sweeps over to enquire, "Haven't I seen you somewhere before, lady?" Tapping her cigarette ash into the palm of her hand she continues, "I never forget a face, you know."

"You'd better forget mine," I think to myself, moving across the room to sit on a derelict couch. She pursues me, sitting beside me, her thigh rubbing mine. I pull my leg away. Undaunted, she says, "Just give me time, lady. I promise you, you'll come back to me." She tries to touch me. I brush her arm away and glare fiercely at her. She rises, moves away, muttering to herself.

Recreation is under way. We have a choice of Ludo or Snakes and Ladders. The tokens are scraps of paper. One woman uses her finger, holding it assiduously to the board while the others move around it to continue the game. For those of us who don't find this sufficiently stimulating, there is the option of TV or "I spy" in the community room. All I can spy in this room are more shabby tables and chairs, a bald carpet, old Afrikaans magazines, and a tired-looking TV. None of this inspires or motivates me to participate. I simply sit and watch the others till the bell sounds again.

On my way out of the community room, I see the nurses closing all the windows and locking all the doors. The clock on the wall reads 4:30 p.m. and the sun is still high in the sky. Inside, it's quickly like a Turkish bath. But no one seems to mind. It's an opportunity to sleep, and all of us are grateful for sleep since sleep, whether natural or induced, alleviates our inner darkness.

I realize it must be suppertime when I see the chairs being placed around the tables again. I hear the rumble of the trolley but, still slow off the mark, I am again last in line. A different nurse is serving this time, and our dislike is immediate, mutual and spontaneous the moment she asks me if I want "*een of twee*?" When I ask her one or two of what she testily replies, "*Lepels sop, mal kop*!" My Afrikaans may be poor, but I can understand "mad head" when I hear it. I contain my anger, say nothing as she serves me one miserable spoonful of grated vegetable soup. Her coarse hands and dirty fingernails seem to emphasize our worthlessness, as does the soup's container—a pail, like you would use to feed pigs. At least this time when I get back to the table, there are still two slices of bread waiting for me.

My tablemates do not remain silent, as they did during lunch. Unlike the patients at the hospital, they don't want to know why I have been admitted; instead they're all eager to share their histories with a newcomer. With no psychiatrist or therapist present, tongues are loose, the language colourful and vulgar. The youngest girl, probably eighteen years old, tells us she is there because she constantly walked on her toes. We ask if this is a mental disorder, but all she can say is that her habit had irritated her parents to the point of having her admitted. When she finishes telling her story, a statuesque lady with porcelain skin, plucked eyebrows, rouged cheeks and ruby, ruby lips, tells us she is a penniless prostitute. She praises the Institution for taking her on a rehabilitation programme. She has a marvellous sense of humour and easily earns our sympathy as her story unfolds.

She had met a suave gentleman at a pub one evening. He promised her a great deal of money for her favours, to which she willingly agreed. On delivering the goods, however, things turned sour. He refused to pay, and so she screamed names at him. He beat her, giving her a black eye and two fractured ribs. Then he tore her wig off her head, tied her to a chair, and ransacked her flat. Taking all her money, before he closed the door he pinned a note to it, "Back in a few days," and made off. Laughing, she describes how she had hobbled and pushed her tied-up body into the kitchen to reach the telephone. Unfortunately she tumbled over the dustbin in the process, hit her shoulder on the open door of the washing machine, and landed face down in the cat's saucer of sour milk. We burst into peals of loud laughter. She adds that the Institution is paying her one Rand a day towards her rehabilitation. "Tiptoes" can't believe it. She sets us off again when she remarks, "Did you say a . . . *Rand?*"

The last one to speak strikes me as truly blue-blooded. She is tall, dignified and has her hair tied back in the neatest bun I have ever seen—not the trace of a hairpin anywhere. She speaks Afrikaans, and stuns me when she says she has been in the Institution for twenty years! "It has been my sanctuary," she adds matter-of-factly. She goes on to tell us that she lost her husband in a car accident, and that her two sons then robbed her of her inheritance, rejecting her in the process. Despite the obvious trauma involved in relating her tale, she remains serene throughout. "I'm happy to potter around the garden, and to attend weekly Mass," she concludes. They all turn to look at me. It seems it's my turn, so I mention that I had run away from the hospital the day before. They all laugh raucously and beg me to tell them more.

It appears that such boisterous behaviour is not common at the Institution, because Sister Coarsehands soon hurries down to our table to investigate. She is given no change from us, however. As at the hospital, there are no squealers. Solidarity reigns supreme among us *mal kops*.

Immediately after supper, chairs are pushed back along the wall, and I arrive at the moment I've been anticipating—the allotment of our medication. We step forward upon hearing our names barked out . . . "Bielovich!" I respond like the rest, without hesitation. I can hardly contain my jubilation as I receive my hormone tablet and *nothing* else! The professor has heard me, and I'm more convinced than ever that my stay is going to be a short one.

I remain seated until the medicine cabinet is locked and wheeled away, happily watching my three table companions go upstairs, while others move off to the community room. I make my way to the dormitory where, for the first time, I see the patients with whom I will be sharing the dorm. Three of the beds are empty, the others are occupied by bodies draped over them in various stages of undress. One woman is standing in her panties, holding one stringy breast shoulder high while she lavishes her diaphragm with cheap-smelling talcum powder. Another has her leg up on the armchair, trying to cut her toenails with an old pair of dressmaking scissors, swearing loudly every time she nicks herself. In the alcove, a plump little lady with small hands and pudgy fingers, wearing a Japanese dressing gown, sits cross-legged, meditating and humming to herself. She must feel my eyes upon her, because her eyes open slowly and she smiles as she says, "My name is Susan and I don't like to talk to anyone." That is fine with me.

I have no intention of undressing in front of everyone, so I make my way down to the ablution block hoping to undress in the bathroom, only to find it locked for the night. I undress with my back to the door in the toilet cubicle, place my clothes in the locker and return to bed. I turn back the crumpled cover and coarse blanket, and lay down on a stiff sheet, staring at the ceiling. My reverie is rudely interrupted by the woman bulging out of her nightdress in the next bed, "Hey, fancy pants, you think you got something we never seen before?" I ignore her, turn on my side, and watch the stars peeping through the gaps between the safety pins which hold the tattered curtains together. I fight to suppress the tide of fear that rises each time I think I have been committed indefinitely to this place.

Having no sleeping pill, tranquillizer or antidepressant, it's a restless night. I get up to go to the bathroom, and, padding around in the half-darkened room in my slippers, I peer at the sprawled and snoring bodies. Deep inside I brood over how I have come to be part of this mass of human misery. The sister comes around a little later, shining her torch in my eyes, but I pretend to be asleep.

Lights come on at 4:45 a.m. and there is a hasty exit from all the beds towards the bathroom. Once again, ignorant of procedure, I am slow to follow, and the nurse marches down towards my bed yelling, "Bielovich! To the bathroom!" I grab my toiletry bag and towel and follow timidly in her bow-legged military steps. Although a queue of miserable women has already formed, she pushes me into its middle and makes her way to the head of the line where she stands guard. No one speaks; a surly silence hangs in the air as we wait our turn. As I draw nearer I see that the door remains open throughout—a shock to my shy disposition. Entering the bathroom, I try to close the door behind me, but "bow-legs" stands against it, solid as the rock of Gibraltar. "You have ten minutes to bath, dress and clean the bath," she pronounces.

At home one of my greatest pleasures was my bath. My bath was where I reflected, relaxed, read, dreamed my dreams. The porcelain bath I now step into has a channel of rust running down its middle, and a dirty low-tide line running all round it. I quickly discover it's over six-feet long when I slither like a piece of cooked macaroni down to the plug, bringing a smirk to the nurse's sour, prunelike face. Undoubtedly a conspiracy exists between the taps: the hot tap spits and bubbles in bursts, while the cold one only dribbles. Stepping out of the bath, crimson-faced in front of all, the words from my obese bedmate—"fancy pants"—come to mind, and I deeply resent this invasion of privacy. There is nothing I can do about it however, and so, like the others, I shuffle off to make my bed, then sit at its foot doing nothing until breakfast.

Having only eaten the leftovers of the mutton stew and "soup" since leaving the hospital, I am famished. With the rumble of the approaching trolley, I am up and rearing to go before grace is even ended. I needn't have bothered. Aside from the lumpy mealie-meal, there is only a tablespoon of coarsely grated cheese to accompany the bread and jam. When I ask Coarsehands if there is anything else, and see the expression on her face for having dared ask, I understand the full measure of Oliver Twist's disgrace. Unlike at the hospital, here there is no "trading." My ravenous stomach continues to grumble.

After breakfast the chairs are rearranged in rows, and I have my first lesson in Afrikaans Psalm singing. Every time Coarsehands walks down my row, I open my voiceless mouth, imitating a far more enthusiastic singer. After a few geriatric exercises, medication is given and once again my name isn't called. Inwardly, I rejoice at my exclusion from the medicine trolley.

Within days I settle into the routine and roster duties of the Institution. When it comes to washing the dishes in a trough, my back objects, so instead I'm assigned to drying countless dishes with only four dish cloths. I must constantly ring them out. Conversation circulates freely in the privacy of the dirty nook of a kitchen, but I rarely speak, and somewhere, in the clouded heel of my mind, I realize that this is not like me.

Though I am not aware of it at the time, the root of this ominous mood shift is that the hospital's steady diet of pills has been cut off overnight. My "cold turkey" has now begun in earnest. Headaches, nausea, the shakes, all overtake me, yet that much I can handle. The alien thing which possesses, devours and regurgitates me as its clone and puppet, I have no control over. My mind and spirit harden by the day.

When Nicky and the girls try to penetrate this hard-shelled "thing" they lovingly called Cookala or Mommy, they become its victims. While they give me only unconditional love, I have only naked hostility to offer them in return. How can I possibly describe to them my new tomb of "nothingness?" In the hospital I had cut myself off from TV, radio, music, people; now I move into a further extension of isolation where I feel time itself has atrophied. My whole life is nothing more than a Pavlovian response. Where sounds of music and nature had nurtured, comforted and inspired me during my previous illnesses, I now resent intrusion of any kind into my hidden world. All physical contact becomes repulsive and abhorrent as a rottenness from my inner core surfaces like a pip from a boil. Everything seems to be rancid, sour, off. Food no longer has flavour on my palate; I simply push lumps of "sameness" through a hole in my face. Eyes which had sparkled, shed tears of joy and sorrow, partaken in the fullness of life, are now vacant pools behind which lays only impenetrable darkness. There is nothing out there, or in here. I am enmeshed in nothing. God is gone! Had He ever been? Did He ever exist? Is this then madness, craziness, insanity? It feels like an interminable winter in hell.

The long summer days crawl by. One morning at breakfast I hear that Christmas is just a few days away, and that some of us will be discharged or given a day pass. I listen to the other patients' excitement and I loathe the lot of them for *feeling* happy. I wish that my already dead body could also be deaf and blind to their natural response. A group of women from some charitable organization comes one afternoon, bearing token gifts for "those poor people who won't be with their families, but are warmly remembered in the heart." I don't even bother to open my gift. Instead I watch the nurses preparing for the big day, cutting countless crinkle-paper streamers, arguing among themselves as to where they are going to hang them in the high-ceilinged room. They settle on draping them over anything they can find. One of the ladies from upstairs comes and sits down at the piano. She begins playing a familiar Christmas carol. I get up and walk away.

I return later, and she is still playing. This time, however, the tune is unknown to me. Despite my mood, the music somehow soothes me, and I stand there in my nightdress for a long time, watching her long, bony fingers draw life from the ivory keys.

Back at my bed, I pin the curtains together and look outside. I see no star in the east, only a supercilious moon looking down at me from another window. I imagine my family excitedly preparing to attend midnight Mass together. "They can have it," I think to myself, "I don't care." Lying in bed, I trash myself over and over again, "You stupid bitch, cow. You belong with the pigs, not them."

Christmas morning the lights come on the same time as usual, but there are no presents waiting at the foot of any bed. Only those who have day passes give cursory seasonal greetings as they head towards the line for the compulsory bath. For me it is just another day. I get up, make my bed, and, for the first time since my arrival, take stock of myself in the cracked mirror. My distorted image bears the mask of tragedy and does little to restore my lost self-respect. My eyes, which had looked haunted when I was suicidal, now are utterly devoid of any expression, just two blue discs with black holes in them. My lustreless hair has grown out chaotically; the skin on my face, arms and legs is taut, dry and scaly. And yet I'm not concerned. Everyone around me looks no better.

Full of Christmas cheer, "Patent Shoes," the woman who never forgets a face, sidles into our dormitory singing, "I wish you a Merry Christmas, I wish you a Merry Christmas." Before she can add, "and a Happy New Year," I tell her to "bugger off," then quickly bundle her out of the room. Lack of goodwill is the order of the day.

Our usual breakfast arrives with a hard-boiled egg thrown in to celebrate the great day, after which friends and family arrive to collect those with day passes. Those remaining behind stand around and watch a nurse prepare the table for Christmas dinner. At home this had always been my forte. With endless trouble I would eagerly set the table, making my own special crackers and all sorts of treats to last throughout the day. "Shove the lot of you, making such a screw up," I now think, watching the others join the tables together.

The horrible plastic tablecloths are covered with white paper, crackers are placed on the side plates, and platters of loaf cuts are placed in the centre. Potato salad, baked beans and beetroot dominate the otherwise sparse table. What makes the meal truly different, however, is that "they" sit down with "us!" Everyone dons party hats, and the dulcet voices of the staff offer us food, glorious food. This certainly is a day of generosity because there are also two packets of Marie biscuits waiting for us at tea-time. Our collective cup runneth over.

But not mine. I remain on the periphery, entombed in solitude, hoping that Nicky and the girls will not come. I don't want to see their smiling faces, hear their Christmas greetings, receive their gifts. Not because I don't love them, or want them, but because I am incapable of giving them anything human in return. My screams are silent, my tears dry, my brain dead. My self-rejection is total. The capacity to feel and express our feelings is what humanizes us, gives us meaning, but I no longer know what it is to feel. *I* myself have no meaning, and Christmas itself is abhorrent to me for this very reason. It shows me the thing *I am not* and my family members are—*normal*. Cancer sounds sweeter to me than that damning word, normal.

From my dormitory window, shortly before afternoon tea, I see them arrive. As usual, Nicky is beautifully dressed. So are the girls in their brightly coloured dresses. They step out of the car, and Nicky gathers the girls to his side and chats to them like a mother hen with her brood of chicks. I see their closeness and hate them all for it. They are my family in name only. Any link or human bond has been devoured by the alien thing that has sucked the fibre from my soul. I do not go out to meet them, hoping they will remember that I had asked them not to come. But they come, bearing gifts and love.

They enter the dormitory all bunched up, everyone wanting to be first to bear-hug and wish me a happy Christmas. I remain seated in the broken armchair. "I told you not to waste your time coming here," I remind them. "I don't want to see anybody. Not even you."

"That's fine with us, Mommy," Cathy says. "*We* want to see you. Christmas wouldn't be Christmas without our being with you."

They speak to me as if everything is normal. "Gee, Mom, midnight Mass was crowded. Granny Roma and Aunty Rose knelt behind us in church. They told us to tell you they're coming to visit you one of these days."

"Tell them not to bother," I respond, shuddering at the prospect. They pretend they haven't heard.

Cathy and Debby speak in the same breath, "We all went to Aunty Margie's for Christmas dinner. Everybody sends their love."

"So what," I think to myself.

Linda places a ribboned cake-box on my bedside cabinet, then lifts the lid. "We brought you a little bit of everything you like, Mommy. Would you like to try one of the mince pies we made especially for you?"

"No thanks," I reply, not even bothering to look inside.

Nicky tries to redeem the ugly moment. He pulls a beautifully wrapped gift out from behind his back and hands it to me with a huge smile on his face, "I've brought you something special, Cookala. Something you have always wanted. Open it and see for yourself."

"I couldn't care what it is you've brought, Nicky. I really don't want it. You can do what you like with it. Take it back home."

"Ahh, come on now, Fel," he replies good naturedly, while he tears open the paper. "Just take a peep. You'll love it."

Grudgingly, I look. It's a camera. I gather it is foolproof, exactly what I had always wanted. But I don't want it now. How could he be so stupid to bring it into this repulsive place? Unperturbed by my behaviour, Nicky points to a magnificent patriarchal jacaranda tree still blooming in all its lilac splendour in the garden and says, "Take a shot of that, Fel."

I look at the tree, breathing life and beauty, and want to punch him. Everything in my life is dead. I am not being facetious when I retort, "Would you also like me to take some photographs of the inmates, Nicky?"

He comes and sits down on the arm of the chair, taking my rough hand into his, and remarks matter-of-factly, "I didn't buy it for here, Fel, but for when you come home." The girls all nod their heads, trying hard to hold back their tears.

"Come home?" I spit at him. "Don't you know yet, I'm never coming home? I'm here for life. I belong here. All shit belongs here! You know I'm shit, you can see it! Why can't you say it? I won't let you go home until you tell me how much you hate me. All of you, do you hear me?" I need them to actually say, "We hate you." I need to discover whether my response will be a "normal" one or not.

Nicky's loving response, "How can we say we hate you, when all we do is love you," denies me the assurance I so desperately seek in my darkness. I beg and plead with them, but all I get back is, "We only love you. We know this isn't the real you." Nicky adds, "Just give yourself time, and you'll soon be back home," I stand up and explode, "Time! There's no such bloody thing as time! Can't you see it's stopped? It's just like me!" Unperturbed, Nicky takes me in his arms and hugs me goodbye. So do the girls. It is the worst Christmas of their lives.

With the horrid day over, I don't want anymore holiday visitors, knowing that I will only reject them. But the first one to ignore my wish for solitude is a friend from school days, one of my bridesmaids, who arrives unexpectedly with her mother. They have come out of friendship and concern, only to be confronted by an alien. I am rude, dogmatic, hostile, treating them as intruders. At one point, Yvonne becomes exasperated with me for trashing myself. "Stop doing this to yourself, Fel. You've always been an example to others. Look at all the good things you've done for the school and in the church over the years. People look up to you. I've known you since grade one. How can you tell me that you hate yourself and everybody else when I know you as a caring and loving person?" She tries hard to pull me back to myself, but she doesn't understand the void I am lost in. Neither do I.

With Christmas now a shadow lying across my past, the spectre of New Year's arises. Having nothing to celebrate, I tell Nicky to accept his brother's invitation to spend the holiday with him, and the family unhappily agrees to do so. The day staff are given the afternoon off, and we are left to our own devices. I spend my time outside, lying on my back on the unmown grass, staring up at the clouds. I used to love creating or deciphering cloud-pictures to suit my mood, but now even the grey, heavy rain-filled clouds, with their feathery fingers gathering and linking up to each other, refuse to respond to my attempt.

I stay out till lock-up time, when our relieving parish priest arrives bearing seasonal greetings. I tell him curtly to go away. I don't need his good wishes or counsel. Although a shy man, he persuades me with Irish charm to sit outside with him under a huge oak tree, where within minutes he opens a festering, raw wound. He dares to speak of the *love* of God. Whose God? Certainly not mine. I don't want to hear anything about this person I had so faithfully and willingly served for as long as I can remember—in the parish, African mission, old-age homes, on the street. I have reached a point where everything I once believed in has been abandoned. I spit it all out, in huge indigestible lumps, hoping he will go home. But his skin is too thick. Even when the sky erupts into thunder, lightning and driving rain and I tell him to go, he remains, inviting me to sit in his car till the rain stops. We climb in and I continue my diatribe against all that is holy, while he sits patiently and listens.

"You say that God is a god of love," I rant. "Well you have to be crazy to believe that rubbish! Do you think He cares a damn about me or what is happening in this hell hole? Don't even answer because I can tell you He doesn't. He is a deaf, blind and dumb God who breaks promises. I was a fool to trust Him. I used to believe in the power of prayer. Not anymore. Let Him find some other sucker. Better still let Him pray for Himself. I'm not having anything more to do with Him. He can go to hell for all I'm concerned!"

"If that's your choice, Felicity, fine," he says. "Hate Him. It will change you, but it will never change Him or how much He loves you."

"How can He love me when I've lost my soul and belong to the devil?" I argue, going round and round in circles while the lightning flashes and thunder crashes all round us. "I am evil incarnate," I tell him. "If I'm not, why have I been cast out?" The priest persistently tries, with great gentleness, to open hell's door, but there is no handle on my side. I hear his words, want to believe them, but all escape is denied.

Before departing he tries one last time to comfort me, saying, "God works in strange ways, Felicity. I don't know why you have to suffer like this, but I am certain the day will come when you will look back on this whole experience as one of personal growth and spiritual enrichment." And the doctors believe I am crazy! "Get out. Leave here and don't ever come and see me again," I tell him in disgust. I go inside, hating myself and the world more than ever. I hope the new year will never come.

But the new year does come. The days pass in total passivity, with no sign that progress of any kind is being made. Pouring tea for myself one Sunday afternoon I look up to see my mother and sister Rosemary arriving. I want to run and hide. I don't want them to see me in my squalor. When they enter the ward I know it must be very traumatic for my mother, but she gives no indication of her feelings, simply saying that I don't belong here but at home. My sister adds that life is beautiful, and I feel outraged. How dare she say such a meaningless thing to me?

The following day, I go walking on my own. Halfway up a small *kopje** I am joined by a young, white-jacketed doctor carrying several files under his arm. He invites me to tell him my story as we sit down on a splintered wooden bench. Unemotionally I tell him how I hate the world, people, God; why I had run away from the hospital. He asks intelligent questions, listens attentively, tut-tutting and nodding his head in understanding, "I know exactly what you're feeling and saying about drugs, Felicity. I've been there. I've experimented with them myself, and with my patients. I tried so many different combinations I had to give up my practise eventually, because I couldn't handle their devastating side-effects. I had all these ants

*hill

crawling inside my head, eating my brains out. It was awful, because they only ate during the day when I was working."

While he is telling me this, an irate, gesticulating nurse calls to us. We walk together down the *kopje* to meet her. "Mr. von Brandis," she yells, "how many times have I told you not to leave block A? Move along now and get back to your ward."

On our way back to the dormitory, the nurse tells me he is a harmless patient who truly believes he was a practising doctor. Until he reached the part about the ants in his head, he was so self-assured that I never knew the difference.

One time on one of my forbidden walks, I leave the big red building behind me and make my way round to the back entrance. Out of nowhere a middle-aged man joins me, then suddenly grabs and kisses me wetly on the mouth. I am revolted, and vow to never venture beyond the periphery again. Nor do I tell the nurse in charge what happened.

It's still January, and I'm working on my cross-stitch cloth in the dining room. A woman of indeterminable age, dressed like a washerwoman, thumps her way down the stairs. With her is a pretty, heavily pregnant young girl. I am wondering when and where the baby will be delivered when she is suddenly, viciously attacked by her older companion. I don't know what provokes it, but the young girl retaliates with the speed of a jungle cat, her fist striking out at the snapping jaw directly in front of her face. One minute the girl is screaming obscenities at the top of her voice, the next minute she is sprawled on the floor. Curling up into a ball, she tries to protect her unborn child from the short, jabbing kicks of size-10 shoes. My maternal instinct aroused, I spring to her defence, push the big hollering cow away, then turn to help the young woman to her feet. I don't even see the blow coming from behind.

The heavy blow from Coarsehands literally lifts me off my feet, and I fly across the floor landing between the legs of a dining-room chair. The noise attracts everyone in the ward. A few male patients passing by outside enter the room, lusting for more blood than my bloodied nose and the young girl's torn, bleeding lip can provide. They yell, "Flatten her, flatten her," and punch their fists into their hands. Pandemonium breaks out, with everyone immediately taking sides. But Coarsehands, filled with power and glory, screams at me, "Bielovich, pack your bags! I'm taking you elsewhere. Troublemakers don't belong here!" The washerwoman is led away by another nurse.

Coarsehands leads me to a new block where I am locked up in a room with a shutter on the door by a nurse who makes Coarsehands appear angelic. Her toxic breath causes me to recoil as she tells me to "get inside and wait," slamming the door behind her. The room is small and windowless. A jagged crack running across the wall smiles cynically at me. The bed against the wall is actually a doctor's examination couch; the cracked imitation leather covering is torn and patched, brittle to the touch. The room's sole other article is a dirty, chipped enamel chamber pot, which even my near-bursting bladder rejects with contempt.

I sit petrified on the bed, dangling my feet, waiting for the nurse to return. I don't wait long. Abruptly the hatch shoots up and she shouts, "Bielovich, stop knocking on the wall!"

"I'm not," I answer timidly.

The hatch shudders as she slams it closed. The door swings violently on its hinges, she enters and steps up to my face, poking her finger painfully into my shoulder. "If I say you are knocking, you are knocking. Do you get it? I tell the doctor who does what around this place, do you understand?"

Even in my numbed state, I understand all too clearly the incredible power she holds over my present and future life. If she chooses to, she can tell the professor and the visiting psychiatrist whatever she likes about me, and they will believe her. I won't be able to defend myself. She is the one in control. I am the prisoner. She is sane. I am crazy. Whatever she says will be the truth and that is all that matters. In this moment I know I have been ultimately betrayed. I followed the advice of the health professionals: "Take as prescribed." And now I have been sentenced and handed over to a system which locks me in a windowless room with a shutter on the door, a room where the obscene two-step dance of normal versus crazy reaches such an absurd frenzy that I am left falsely accused, and completely and utterly powerless. This indeed *is* the Judas room. She slams the door shut again.

Outside I hear her conversing with someone. From what I overhear I gather there isn't a bed for me. They come to a decision and the door is wrenched open again and I am told to follow. I emerge subdued and docile. Suppertime has passed and I am hungry but say nothing as I am led into a corridorlike ward with five beds, all occupied by reclining patients. Leading me to a makeshift bed at the far end of the room the nurse loudly announces to them, "This woman started a fight in A Block. Leave her alone." My reputation as a troublemaker thus established, I unpack, change and crawl into bed. No one speaks the entire time. Sleep does not come until the early hours.

Frightened into submission, I soon learn to pay obsequious deference to the nurse and her eager lackeys. They all seem to have a need to show us *mal kops* that they are the bosses, and an all-consuming fear makes me putty in their hands. Like Alice through the looking glass, I am trapped, looking helplessly through the Judas window.

A couple of days later, I find the courage to ask what has happened to the young girl, and the whereabouts of the woman who caused all the trouble. Grudgingly, the nurse informs me that the baby had been delivered that night in the hospital and has been put up for adoption. The young mother is to return to the Institution during the week. The troublemaker is where she rightfully belongs—"in 12B." I have heard many different stories about this ward—most of them featuring its extreme notoriety—and I want to see it for myself. I ask the nurse if this is possible. She refuses outright, saying people only go there if they do something *very bad*—no further elaboration offered. Her clipped reply only works to increase my bizarre and inexplicable curiosity about this ward, and in the wake of our conversation I am more determined than ever to see it. I decide to do something to warrant entry.

I steal a patient's radio. The expected outcry results, and the hunt is on to find the criminal. I initially enjoy the hue and cry. Coarsehands is all wound up, searching feverishly through our lockers. A viciously pulled drawer from a dresser falls on her clumsy foot, and I silently rejoice. Her neck is as red as a turkey's and in that moment I want to see her anger, hear her anger. Finally I defiantly own up, collecting the radio from the kitchen where I have hidden it. I thrust it into her outstretched hand. Turning it over, her beady eyes scrutinize the object. She is trained to deal with patients like me, and, sharp as a razor, she says, "Bielovich, you think this will get you sent to 12B, don't you? Well it won't. Remember it's me who gets what I want, not you. But come along and see where people who play games like you can go."

I follow her outside, and she leads me to another building, which we enter through a side gate. She takes me down a never-ending corridor, all the while telling me quite chattily that no one, but no one, not even the "rubbishy ones" like me, gets the better of her. She has karate training, I am told, making her invulnerable. We pass a vacant little chapel on our way "for those who need to pray."

Without a flicker of emotion, or interrupting our conversation, Coarsehands opens a door and orders me inside. The moment I enter I know I am in Dante's Inferno, a place of the damned. Like a swarm of bees, eight women climb over their low divan beds, screaming and spitting obscenities. Though it is midday, they are all still in their nightgowns. Their eyes are lustreless, the odd one blackened, and their inner torment is as palpable as the stale, rancid air in the windowless room. A naked bulb hangs from the ceiling, reminding me, absurdly, of the chicken coop from years ago on my uncle's farm. Their domino-eyed, rotund keeper approaches us belligerently, wanting to know why I have come. With imaginative embellishments Coarsehands tells her how I have fought with a young pregnant woman, stolen a radio from another and asked to *stay* in 12B. Before I can present my version, Dominos asks, "Is this where you really want to come, Bielovich?" *Is it?* The scene fills me with horror, wrenching my soul from its bearings.

We are interrupted by two venom-spewing women. They come directly up to me, their jabbing fingers poking into my ribs. "Get her out of here!" they scream. "We don't want this bitch in here with us. Get her out!" Dominos delivers a karate blow to the nearest one. Like curs they retreat over the beds, huddling in a corner. I am thoroughly cowed, and, seeing the smirking faces of Coarsehands and Dominos, I know my response is precisely what they expected, wanted. It secures and guarantees their ownership over me.

Before leaving the hellish room, Coarsehands shows me a dark little hole which serves as the ward's dining room. It makes me shudder. Then she leads me to an "exercise area" directly off the dining room. I feel myself being torn asunder. It is a literal cage; the only thing preventing it from being part of a zoo is the absence of raw meat on the hard, uneven ground. A deeply worn, narrow path on the periphery underlines for me the isolation and loneliness of the internees. Does any behaviour deserve captivity like this? Every fibre of my body screams that I will never, never, *never* step out of line again. From that moment on I am bound over to the Institution, totally subservient. Whatever is asked I will do. Just don't ever put me in this place.

That night, and several thereafter, hideous images of writhing bodies, mangled hair and shrewish screams make me repeatedly question my own sanity. I withdraw further and further into my own darkness. I am in hell.

My new subservience rewards me a fortnight later. I am returned to my original ward. Coarsehands greets me with a knowing smile and wagging finger, but I need no reminders. I know my place. When "Tiptoes" comes over and introduces me to her friend Sara, I feel I have come home. The safety pins on the curtain and my lumpy bed are enough to secure me a good night's sleep. I even welcome the familiar watery stew.

Two days later, Nicky's cousin, Marko, and his wife, Joan, up from Durban for a wedding, arrive unexpectedly. They have spent three hours driving around searching for the Institution and, to my dismay, are let in after hours. I am in my nightdress but hurriedly dress and meet them in the dining room, where several other patients are playing Ludo. Marko comments how pleasantly surprised he is that no one seems to mind being in such a place. They bring me an exquisite little Coalport china urn filled with pot-pourri, and I want to laugh at the incongruity of this little work of art in such a godforsaken place. I murmur an ungracious thank you, barely uttering another word. After they leave, with Joan looking very upset, I gently place the little urn on the horrid chipped enamel locker next to my bed. Despite my lack of gratitude, holding the urn causes me to feel a nostalgic link with my past.

Time continues to drag, and my cross-stitch cloth becomes the only tie connecting my past and present. As long as I keep that cloth with me wherever I go, I know Felicity once existed. When the Anglican or Croatian priests visit, they don't understand how completely lost I am in myself, and that it is impossible for me to respond to the blooming hibiscus they regularly point out. But they certainly hear my bitter response whenever they mention God. And yet, even in my barren state, their patience, nonjudgmental attitude and understanding make a grudging impression on me.

Early in the new year the psychiatrist thinks I am ready for a day pass. What makes him think this I cannot imagine, but as usual I follow orders. Nicky arrives full of smiles to take me home for the day. I have nothing to smile about. I don't belong with people who laugh, share, speak. I want to be treated like the dirt I am. Mine is not a state of self-pity, but one of total, absolute self-rejection, a rejection which demands reciprocity. My family is incapable of delivering that. Instead they give love, attention, care and laughter, and so their efforts pass me by like flour through a sieve. The roast leg of lamb, honey-gold roast potatoes, succulent vegetables and exotic desserts they serve me cannot induce my taste buds to respond. My taste buds are barren, like me. Even my cat, which in days past never left my side, is rejected. Our traditional Sunday high tea, which once knitted us together in harmony, now simply reinforces my perception that I no longer belong. For me the whole exercise is a miserable failure, and I'm pleased when the day comes to an end. I leave the house disoriented, more convinced than ever that I belong in a mental institution. When we arrive there I feel at home. I no longer have to try to be Felicity. I can just be a blob, a nobody.

Nevertheless, the visit deeply unsettles me. Despite everything, I know in my heart that home is where I belong, and feelings of frustration and anger begin to gnaw at my insides. I become aggressive. My elbows become my mouth. I push to the head of the food queue, force my way into the bathroom for the first bath, defying the nurse to stop me. Even 12B no longer frightens me. I will take charge of myself!

One afternoon, filled with seething animal anger, I march into the community room, pick up a chair, and repeatedly strike the TV screen with it. But no matter how hard I hit it, the screen won't break. A passing nurse sees me in the act and pulls me away. She sits me down in a nearby chair and tells me she understands my frustration, my need to lash out. She surprises me by adding that my behaviour is a progressive sign. It conveys to her that my dormant feelings are emerging, becoming real, that my capacity to express a genuine feeling is returning. It doesn't matter if that feeling is hate, anger or guilt, she adds, it is real, and that's what counts. I don't know whether to believe her. I certainly want to.

Days pass, and a kernel of hope, planted by the passing nurse, slowly penetrates my subconscious, and my anger and frustration begin to dissipate. A childhood friend visits and is not subjected to verbal abuse. She takes me back in time, recalling incidents I have lost in the fog. "Do you remember the time that we were caught stealing fruit in that mango grove? The day the engine driver stopped the train and reported us to my father for not getting off the line when he blew his hooter? The night we jumped into our beds fully dressed so nobody would guess it was us who had hypnotized the neighbour's daughter?" Listening to her recall the magic moments we had shared over the years, I recall that her birthday is falling this week and remark that it will be the first birthday I won't share with her. I wish her well.

Like Linus with his blanket, I continue to drag my cross-stitch cloth everywhere. We are bound together like Siamese twins. Sitting in the dining room early one morning with my cloth, I feel the urge to telephone my husband. I walk to a call-box on the grounds, on my way noticing the beautiful hibiscus blooms for the first time. Nicky comes on the line sounding happy and excited to hear my voice but, while he is speaking, I feel the pain of darkness circle and enshroud my mind. I hang up on him and retreat back inside.

Seeing the professor later that day, I mention the telephone call to my husband, but think it might be a figment of my imagination or a delusion, as it all seems so vague. Fortunately he takes me seriously and checks out my story, confirming that my telephone call is a *fact*. He is delighted, saying this is a sign of progress, that there is "light at the end of the tunnel." He is certain my depression will lift, but he can't say when.

I have only seen a psychiatrist twice since my arrival, but after my conversation with the professor I see one on a regular basis—Dr. Smythe. I am surprised when we meet. He looks young enough to be my son. He tells me he is in his final year at university, and adds that the more I can tell him about myself the better. I like his approach, but my initial faith is shaken when he prescribes medication—lithium—a drug, he tells me, used in the treatment of manic and recurrent depression. I have been totally drug-free for two months and I am very scared to go back on them. He explains how carefully the drug is monitored and, having no personal control, I acquiesce.

The lithium makes no tangible difference. I stay exactly where I am—nowhere. As the weeks pass a helpless despair begins to press me further and further down into a black hole. The despair manifests itself in every waking moment. I feel the net drawing tighter and tighter. I am bereft, barren and without hope, resigned to being trapped in the Institution forever. I feel so desolate that even my cross-stitch no longer offers any solace. Felicity is gone. She is lost forever.

I take my cloth upstairs and give it to a woman who has always admired it. This area is out of bounds and I've never been up here before, but I don't care. I notice though, that compared with the crying and shouting I have so often overheard downstairs, these patients are more animated and positive than we are. "Tiptoes" is lying on her bed reading, and she's quite touched when I give her my travel Scrabble. Going over to the young, childless mother, I place my wedding ring on her finger and tell her she can have it. She's overjoyed. Dejectedly, I make my way downstairs and step outside.

Walking around the garden, looking up at the dry *kopjes*, biblical texts drift in and out of my mind. The words of the Psalmist, "I will look unto the hills from whence my help will come," repeat themselves time and time again in my head. Angrily I raise my fist to the hills, berating the Psalmist's foolish optimism with my newly acquired gutter-talk. I work myself into such a frenzy that I fail to see a large rock in front of me. I fall over it, sprawling over other rocks as I struggle to break my fall, hitting my head in the process.

Still swearing vociferously, I rise gingerly to my feet, wondering if I have caused further injury to my fused back or pelvis. But, apart from a bloodied knee and a grazed ear, I am fine. Then, as I dust myself off, I feel something strange, almost indescribable happening inside my head. There is a tingling sensation, as if my scalp is being peeled back like an orange skin. I can feel a certain pressure being taken off the back of my head, almost hear the "crunch" as everything seems to settle back into its rightful place. There is definitely something real and tangible happening inside my head. I can *feel* it.

Suddenly, my thoughts begin to clear. Like a jigsaw puzzle,

pieces begin to fall into place. I focus on my surroundings, asking myself what I am doing here. Everything looks so ugly. I don't belong here. Why are people walking around this place doing nothing? Why should I be drying dishes when I have a dishwasher at home? Suddenly I know I don't want to stay here—not another day, not another minute.

I recall that our daughter Cathy is engaged, and I have a wedding to organize, a dress to make, so many things to do. I have no time to waste. I have purpose, vision! I want to go home—home. I know where I belong. I know who I am. I am Felicity.

I hobble off to the nurse in charge, a huge smile on my face, startling new thoughts jumping around in my head. The nurse, seeing me, immediately leaves off what she is doing. She comes down the stairs, arms outreached, "Mrs. Bielovich, what has happened to you? I've never seen you smile before. You look wonderful." Before I can answer, she loudly exclaims, "Just wait until the professor sees you!" Linking her arm through mine, she hurries me off to Professor Stack, chatting happily all the way. I am no longer a goat being led on a string but a happy terrier straining at the leash.

The moment we enter his room the professor jumps up and comes over to me, takes my hand and says, "I don't even have to ask why you're here, Mrs. Bielovich. Your face says it all. This is the day we've waited and hoped for. You've broken through! I'm very, very happy for you." When he adds proudly, "I never believed you belonged here in the first place," I feel ten-feet tall. My heart almost bursts when he continues, "Why don't you phone your husband from my office and give him the good news for yourself? Tell him there are no psychological tests or checks to be done and that if he can, he can come and fetch you immediately." He mentions just one proviso to my release. I must report to an outside psychiatrist on a monthly basis for monitoring. I comply willingly.

Eagerly I try to contact members of my family from the professor's office, but no one is home. Finally, after a multitude of fruitless calls, I locate Cathy. My heart jumps with excitement when she comes on the line, "Good morning. This is 55-2562. Cathy Bielovich speaking."

My words tumble out, "Cathy, it's Mommy here. I can't get hold of Daddy anywhere and I've just been told I can go home." She can't believe me. "No, not just for today, darling. Forever! The professor says you can come and fetch me right now. I really am better." I hear her intake of breath, "I'm on my way, Mom!" and the click of the receiver as she promptly drops it.

I hurry back into the dormitory, seeing everything with different eyes now. I see it in all its ugliness and feel very sorry for all the patients resting on their beds. I can't wait to put the whole experience behind me. I leave the building and stand outside, anxiously awaiting Cathy's arrival.

Her little red car races up the driveway, comes to a screeching halt outside the building. She is absolutely beautiful, her face transfigured as she comes towards me, open-armed, and we hug each other. I am overcome by the joy of feeling her in my arms.

We dash inside with a suitcase. "We're not unpacking this lot when we get back home, Mommy," Cathy says, throwing my clothes in with happy abandon. "We certainly don't need any reminders of this place." Giving me a questioning look she remarks, "By the way, Mom, I see you are not wearing your wedding ring. Where is it?"

"I gave it away earlier this morning, Cathy," I reply. "I didn't think I would need one anymore. I also gave away my travel Scrabble and Irish linen tablecloth. I honestly thought I would never leave this place."

"Mom, they are yours and belong to you," she says agitatedly. "Think what Daddy will feel like when he knows you gave your ring away. I'm going to get them back. You're not going home without your wedding ring." She runs upstairs, returning with the ring and cloth in her hand in a matter of minutes. Concerned as to how she managed to obtain their return so promptly, I ask her what she had said or done. Without hesitation she answers, "I told them you didn't know what you were doing and that you had changed your mind. The young girl was a bit sticky with returning your ring, but I told her it rightfully belonged to you and took it off her finger myself." I slip the ring back onto my finger, grateful to have it back.

Without a backward glance, Cathy hurries me to the car and we drive away through the open gates. My eyes remain steadfastly focused on the road ahead. She places her hand over mine, never letting go, and reassures me the whole way home that everything is going to be fine. Despite my trembling heart, I believe her.

CHAPTER FOUR

Through Night's Door

The whole way home I greedily take in my surroundings. Having been blind to everything for nearly six months, the fiery blaze of the glorious summer countryside, the mackerel sky, sear into the depth of my being. This is my land. But, as the kilometres slip away behind us, so too does my anticipation and excitement. By the time we turn into our drive I feel a sense of unreality. There's no one to greet Cathy and myself, because no one has been told of my return. The house is quiet and deserted.

We let ourselves in and it's like stepping into a time warp. I walk around the rooms, looking at and touching the objects which so personalize my home. Externally, everything appears to be exactly where I had left it. Yet, internally, I know things are very, very different. I feel like a visitor in my own home. Cathy senses my uncertainty. "It's so great to have you home again, Mom. I still can't believe you're home for good. Just wait till the others find out," she says, hugging me to herself. "If you want to come with me now to fetch Debby from the convent in Springs and give her the greatest surprise of her life, you're welcome," she adds, looking at her watch, "otherwise you can stay at home, contact Daddy and give him the surprise."

"What a great idea," I answer enthusiastically. "That's just what I'll do. I'll call him."

She walks to the sink, fills the kettle with water, and says in a mothering sort of way, "What do you say that before I go, we have a good, strong cup of tea?" I like the sound of that.

Watching her make the tea, I notice for the first time the beauty and delicacy of our porcelain teapot and cups. I've become accustomed to a much coarser variety for the past five months. "Now, don't you worry about anything," she says when tea is over. Everything is under control. I'll be back sooner than you think."

When she is gone, like a stranger, I wander into my bedroom. The first thing I see is our neatly made gabled double bed, stirring all sorts of feelings within me. This bed holds my history from the age of twenty when I first came to it with stars in my eyes. In it our four beautiful daughters were conceived. It embraced the six of us every Sunday morning, heard our laughter, accepted our tears. But then, remembering how I had contemplated suicide in it, I'm abruptly repulsed. How can I possibly get back into this same bed tonight, as if nothing has happened. Turning away in apprehension, I see myself in the mirror. I take a long, hard look, shaken and ashamed at my reflected image. I look worse than any of the psychiatric patients I had seen in the bathroom on that first morning in the hospital. I am a replica of the wild washerwoman at the Institution. Five months away from my sheltered environment has left a lasting mark on me—straggly hair, roughened hands, parchment face. Opening my make-up drawer, I see a variety of "war paints" and feel only confusion. I don't know where to begin. I apply a little blush, eye shadow and lipstick, but a tart stares out of my mirror at me. I wash it all off.

At least I can change the dress I've virtually lived in at the Institution. I open my wardrobe, and the selection is immediately daunting. This is my first real decision in five months. I want to wear everything at once! I choose one of my favourite frilly blouses but, like the make-up, it somehow looks incongruous on me. I try something else on but it's wrong too. Finally I settle for a simple skirt and blouse. But even now I'm not comfortable; one part of me feels like Felicity; the other still feels confused, uncertain, alien.

I hear the front door opening. I run up the passage and into Deborah's open arms shouting, "I'm home, Debs! Mommy's home for good!" We both begin crying. My two other daughters, Elizabeth and Linda, arrive together during the afternoon for another emotional reunion. I feel like a lost sheep rewelcomed to the fold.

Everyone takes it in turns to try and track down Nicky. While waiting, I telephone my mother, who arrives within minutes. Words are unnecessary. She's like a big mother hen taking me under her wing.

My ears prick up hearing the familiar sound of Nicky's meat truck coming up the drive. The front door slams, and I go to him. He's standing in the hall with a smile lighting up his face like the sun. He can't really believe it's me back home. We embrace, and only after much hugging, laughing and talking is he truly convinced. Only two days earlier I'd been hostile, an inwardly unrecognizable being. Now here stands his Cookala, as if it had all been a hideous nightmare.

We all crowd into the kitchen in search of food. Anyone seeing or hearing us would think we've hit the lottery jackpot. And we have! We are a family again. The afternoon turns into a very special, raucous, intimate evening. Questions fly to and fro as I try to catch up with all the news of the past five months. Now that I have at last returned home, I remind them of our Black Christmas and ask their forgiveness. I receive a simple, graceful reply: "There is nothing to forgive." No recriminations, only a reaffirmation of their love. My family's unconditional love is an incarnate experience for me; wrapping myself in its healing balm, I feel as though I am taking on new life. The sweetest sounds to my ears all evening are the terms I had once considered mundane: "Mommy, Darling, Cookala, Fel." They are my names. They are me. I am real.

The evening draws to a close and I move off to have my bath. A long lost pleasure unfolds. Standing in the doorway, my eyes take in the beautifully curtained window, the spotless bath, the shower, the pedestalled hand basin, the huge unspeckled mirror. This little paradise is all mine; I don't have to share it with anyone. Gently, I close the door, savouring my privacy. With childlike senses I see, feel, touch as if for the first time. I caress the leaves of the love plants, touch the fragrant soaps, open the stoppers of unguents and lotions, breathing in their fragrance. Slowly I undress, watching how quickly the bath fills with glorious bubbles under the pressure of the mixer tap opened to full throttle. I climb in, lay back and indulge myself with every hedonistic pleasure I can lay hand to. Climbing out of the bath, I dry myself with soft towels, curl my toes into the bath mat like a kitten kneading its mother.

Emerging from my indulgence, I climb happily into my double bed. I slip blissfully between silky sheets and beneath a soft duvet, snuggle up against my husband's body. It is a precious, healing, tender moment.

Waking at 7 a.m., a tea tray on my bedside table, I realize the previous day is not a figment of my imagination. It is real and for always. I lie there in bed, thinking about the daily joys and privileges I had once taken for granted, lost and now regained. It is heady, intoxicating stuff. For the first time I realize the tremendous fortune and power that is again mine to control on a *daily* basis. Pondering this personal power, my life takes on a whole new texture. Everything is suddenly prefixed with *I*. I can map out my day. I can choose when to have my bath, turn out the light, change my bed, switch on and select a radio or TV programme. I can have a swim, read a book, go for a walk. I can make myself a cup of tea *or* coffee, visit a friend, go to a movie. My options and choices are unlimited, free of any constraint. I can do anything, something, nothing! I, Felicity, own this day and every other day in my life. I am ecstatic and have to share this newfound wealth with someone, so I invite my cat, Tiger, to join me on the bed, serving him his milk in a fine porcelain saucer.

Watching Tiger cleaning his whiskers, I also realize this newly discovered fortune should be spent wisely and not squandered. Active community involvement, participation in the real world, leaving the sidelines and picking up threads of friendships which have grown slack during my journey down . . . suddenly it dawns on me—I have become quite accustomed to and secure in my routine as a patient. My euphoric mood tapers down like a dying candle. All sense of intoxication and freedom quickly deserts me and is replaced by a disturbing fear. I am *scared*, scared to go out there. I'm scared of what people will say or think—I imagine myself ducking in and out of shops trying to avoid contact with people I know. I'm suddenly awash in undercurrents of guilt, shame and embarrassment.

Believing the church is a place of sanctuary, I decide to attend with the family to thank God for his generosity in restoring me to life. Before doing this, however, I take myself firmly in hand. I go for a facial and have my hair restyled and colour-rinsed. Staring at my restored image in the mirror, I realize that the repair has succeeded externally, but internally it has done very little. I still feel very afraid. I confide my fears to the family, and so they form a small bodyguard around me as we enter the church. Two daughters kneel in front, two behind, and my husband alongside. The odd pat on the back, a glance, a squeeze of the shoulder, gives me constant reassurance and comfort. When, at the end of Mass the priest says, "Go in peace," I want to believe him, but as I step outside again I feel more like going to pieces.

In the following days I wonder constantly if my recovery is total and permanent, and my emotional soil is particularly fertile for seeds of doubt. I am afraid to look back or analyse anything too deeply, and so I become driven by a sense of urgency to keep moving forward, forward, forward. I realize how emotionally fragile I am and how the support of my family is absolutely crucial. Though I'm not suicidal, I long for respite from my doubts. I can't help wondering about the millions of people who have little or no support to fall back on. How many of them must fall back into the abyss for this very reason?

During this first difficult month at home we celebrate our twenty-fourth wedding anniversary. It is a strange day for me. One part of me is overcome by Nicky's symbolic gift—an enchanting Royal Doulton sylphlike figurine holding a little white dove, wings spread ready for flight, in her open-palmed hand. He quietly explains that it represents me setting myself free forever. The other part of me, yearning to be free, still feels as if an invisible barrier lies between us, because I am still plagued daily, sometimes hourly, by recurring doubts about my true mental state.

I feel a desperate need to set myself free of the past. If I am to succeed in my new life, I believe I must completely disassociate myself from the turmoil of all that has happened. With unresolved anger, self-hatred and guilt, I set out on a mission to destroy every sentimental thing connected with my past. Ruthlessly I search out all my keepsakes, certificates, commendations, anything which gives a clue or bears testimony to the hard-working, caring person I had once pretended to be. I have to bury the Felicity whose life had been a sham. In the purge, I include fifteen years of irreplaceable "wisdom" letters I had received from an eighty-year-old priest/mentor/friend. Everything and anything with my name on, I consign to the bin.

It is a near-fatal mistake. The aftermath of this mission is a feeling of utter disconnectedness. I now no longer know what is true or false about myself. Now instead of being lost in the Institution I find myself totally lost at home. My so-called freedom creates difficulties I could never have anticipated. Having been under the yoke of orders for five months, I have lost my organizational skills and no longer know how to plan the day. I have no purpose, direction, vision and, worst of all, no destination. Suddenly I find myself a stranger to everything happening around me.

Not having listened to the radio, read a newspaper, or watched TV since leaving home, I sit quietly, in ignorant silence as the family animatedly discusses current events around the dinner table. Watching them interrelate so candidly I feel like a dropped stitch in an otherwise splendid garment. I know I am welcome as a part of the whole, but I don't know how to pick myself up and rejoin it. They all seem to have forged such close bonds during my absence. When I see how capably they carry out *my* jobs—organizing the meals, telling Nicky what meat to send from the shop, buying the groceries, doing the baking, sorting the wash, serving him dinner, choosing the wine—I'm shocked to realize I have lost my once pivotal role. I am dispensable. I don't resent their newly found independence and maturity, I respect it. But it fosters a feeling within me that no matter how much I am wanted, I am no longer *needed*. The only life I have known is service to my family, and now all of a sudden my service isn't necessary anymore. They are fine on their own, perhaps even better off without me.

This also includes the kitchen, where I had once reigned supreme. Where once I'd been able to serve a four-course meal with clockwork precision, I now find getting a simple meal together a nightmare. I am totally out of sync. Meat and vegetables arrive at the table either overdone or underdone, or not at all. More often than not my once highly praised flaky pastry and scones discreetly disappear into the yawning dustbin. I can't seem to do anything right.

One morning when the Croatian priest drops over for a visit, I speak to him about my ineptitude, lack of direction and purpose. He explains the art of *polako, polako* (slowly, slowly) to me. He suggests I try to rediscover an area in my life where I had felt competent, confident and unthreatened, and make it a starting point.

I choose sewing. I have long neglected this hobby as my depression eroded all inclination to do anything, but, taking the priest's advice, I buy metres and metres of material. I return home and set to churning out skirts and tops for the girls. As I refamiliarize myself with the mechanics of my sewing machine, the seed of confidence grows. I try planting the seed in other impoverished areas. My memory seems particularly impaired and my concentration span extremely short, so I improve these abilities by studying news reports, statistics, times and titles of forthcoming TV programmes, and actually remembering announcers' names. In the evening, standing in front of the mirror, I verbalize the day's harvest and discover to my satisfaction that *polako, polako*, the seed is truly germinating elsewhere as well.

Having always shared a very close relationship with my mother, I confide these small victories to her. She is delighted but disturbs me when she says matter-of-factly, "I'm seventy-nine years old, darling. I'm not going to live forever. You have to consider what you are going to do with your life when I'm not here for you to visit every day."

These feelings are only amplified when, sitting outside at the swimming pool a few days later watching Elizabeth tanning, I cautiously mention to her that there were times when I experienced very strange feelings inside my head. I try, at great length, to clarify these feelings, while she listens patiently. But then she stands, adjusts her bikini and says, "You'd better find something to do with your life *now*, Mom. We may not be at home next time around." My blood runs cold. My stomach churns. I want to be sick. Panic breaks out. I am a wife and mother. If anyone knows that, she does. How dare she, a slip of a girl, a highly qualified social worker to boot, tell me, her mother, to get out there and do something with my life! I resent her shaking my cage. Outwardly calm, I make my way inside, heart pounding.

But instinctively I know she is right. I simply don't want to hear it. It's simply too painful to have it confirmed that *I* am responsible for my own life, that decisions and choices lay with *me*. Whichever way I argue with myself it always came back to the fact that the solution lies in my hands. I will somehow have to reconstruct myself. But how?

There is a sense of urgency—I have to do something *now*. This simple three-letter word, 'now,' induces in me indescribable fear. It brings back the childhood memory of standing at the end of a swimming pool, with my father urging me over and over again to dive in. Eventually I had done it and loved it.

So I dive in again. I decide to join the International Training in Communication (ITC) organization. The night of my first meeting

I want to turn back in the car park, but I give myself a little pep talk and timidly enter the library theatre. A friendly young woman immediately introduces herself and helps me; the meeting is called to order and the programme is under way. I'm very impressed with the confidence of the speakers, the interesting topic and the well-run meeting, but I keep a low profile, and this is in turn respected by the members. Although I am informed that I can hold visitor status for several weeks, I nervously sign up. I know if I don't, I will never return.

My first month at home is drawing to a close and, honouring the professor's proviso, my husband and I go to the out-patients' clinic in a neighbouring town to see a psychiatrist. The first thing I notice as we enter the modern building is an obscenely large arrow with "Psychiatric Patients" boldly printed on it. We enter a large waiting-room filled with patients, and I feel an instant gnawing anxiety within myself. I haven't come to confirm a physical illness or cure a symptom but to have a mental assessment. Am I in for another digging session? Will this psychiatrist also try to pigeon-hole, label, humiliate me?

My disturbing thoughts are broken as someone nudges me hard in the ribs, and a guttural female voice booms, "What are you here for? Is it for depression? What tablets are you taking? Have you seen this shrink before?" Before I can answer she spits out details of her suicide attempt, with the heated velocity of a rocket being launched into outer space. At ever-increasing decibels I hear all the sordid details of her alcoholic husband's infidelity with a conniving young "bitch" who, given half a chance, she will murder with her own bare hands. Looking at her massive proportions and paddle-sized hands, I believe she could.

This outburst sets off the man sitting opposite me. He goes on ad infinitum about his personal history, striking a chord within me when he mentions the name of the pills I'd been on. Listening to these patients comparing stories and symptoms, I quickly realize how many others are still taking the drug. But, as at the hospital, I remain on the periphery, never mentioning that it had also been prescribed for me, with devastating effects. Instead I ponder the nature of depression and come to the sad conclusion that it is a misunderstood, pariahlike illness which separates and alienates people, both from themselves and their family. It is an illness which rarely evokes compassion; in fact it often elicits the reverse.

In my case it has proved far worse than any physical illness. It has corroded and eaten into the very core of my psyche and emotional well-being. It had destroyed my will to live, brought about abhorrent behavioural changes.

Still deep in thought, I hear my name being called. Nicky and I stand and follow a buxom sister down a passage into a small, clean boxlike room containing a wooden table-cum-desk cluttered with shabby brown files. The buckled and bent steel filing cabinet standing in the corner literally bulging with files causes me to wince. Surely not every inhabitant in the town is sick in the head. We sit down and I see my open file, a page of clearly visible writing indicating that the psychiatrist is already familiar with my story and the fact that I am taking lithium.

Ill at ease, I sit down opposite Dr. van Zeale, a man in his late thirties who is doodling on his blotter. His long, straggly unwashed hair, pushed behind his ears, hangs limply on an open-necked shirt which screams for a bleaching agent. His face is deeply acne-scarred. Dragging himself up from his slouching position, he leans back repeatedly clicking his ball-point pen like a cigarette lighter. I answer a few preliminary questions as to how I am coping, remarking that it is easier getting off the world than back on to it, but that I'm making progress. Apparently this is all he needs hear from me, because all questions are then directed to my husband. Am I crying much, edgy, irritable, restless? Am I more balanced, sleeping properly, in control? Is there anything he would like to add about my behavioural state?

They talk about me as if I am invisible and I realize, that even as an out-patient, I have only observer status. My opinion is not called for, and any contribution I make to the discussion is deemed minimally worthwhile. I feel demeaned and humiliated. At the conclusion of their exchange, I'm stunned to hear him prescribe more pills, in addition to the lithium I am on. I question their purpose, he ignores me, turning to my husband and explains, "The pills are to keep your wife stable." Querying what they are, Nicky is told, "You have nothing to worry about. I am taking six of them myself every day, they're perfectly safe." Nicky is made responsible for seeing that I take the pills, and he tells me to return the following month for a reassessment. Once more the *doctor* has spoken. I am back on pills.

As instructed, my husband becomes my diligent keeper, believing that he is helping to prevent my returning to the Institution. I quickly come to believe he is doing me a disservice in ministering the poison. Within a fortnight strange and unsettling things begin happening again. One night I am driving the car on the way home from a friend's when suddenly a panic-attack assails me. Overpowering fear from nowhere jolts through me. My hands and legs shake violently. I frantically pull over and come to a stop in the emergency lane. My mouth quivers and tears well up in my eyes. I'm lost, confused; I don't know what's happening to me or what to do. Then, suddenly all the symptoms fade and disappear. I wait fifteen minutes, then cautiously drive off again.

A week later I am in a restaurant with Cathy and our future in-laws, enjoying a glass of wine, when, out of the corner of my eye, I see them shrinking. A minute later they grow taller. My stomach muscles contract and I taste the raw fear in my dry mouth. I excuse myself, walk unsteadily to the bathroom and look at myself in the mirror. I see the haunted look back in my eyes. I feel the old terror and restlessness returning.

I make my way back to the table, badly shaken. I sit down and now I feel as if I am somehow elevated, sitting high above everyone else. Conversation seems to float up to and around me. I finish off my glass of wine, hoping to calm myself down, but the alcohol only makes things worse. Trying to distract myself from what is happening inside my head, I cross to the salad bar. On my return Cathy gives me a penetrating look. I'm afraid she suspects something is wrong, and my suspicion is right; as I take my seat she comes and leans over me whispering agitatedly, "Go and put some lipstick on; do something with your face. Join in the conversation. Don't just sit here staring. *Do something*, Mommy."

All I can do is pray that I will somehow stay glued together for the rest of the evening. It's a tremendous strain forcing myself to make small talk when all I want to do is run outside and scream. Finally the evening comes to an end and we arrive home. I run to my bedroom, greedily swallowing my pills, hoping they will make my alarming symptoms go away. But they don't.

Two days later I am sitting outside in the garden celebrating a family dinner. I step inside to fetch a platter of savories, and, as I lift the platter I am assailed by tremors throughout my entire body. My tongue feels thickened. I have to get my pills. On my way I peer out the window, seeing everyone sitting relaxed under the thatch. They are all laughing, enjoying themselves, while I am losing my head. I must be crazy. They don't know, thank God. A new terror grips me. What will happen to them, to me, if they find out? They must never find out. Never.

Somehow I hang in for the rest of the afternoon, but that night I don't sleep at all as my fevered and tortured mind travels back down that frightening road to the place of my entombment. Is this where I will live out the rest of my life? Where does madness come from? Is it genetic? Will my death certificate state madness as the cause of my demise? Will this be the legacy my children will inherit? Am I to blame for it? Questions swirl about unanswered. My mind feels as if it is occupied by an octopus, as coiled tendrils squeeze out a kaleidoscope of grotesque images, with me always at the centre. Feeling the door of my mind closing I pull back sharply and tell myself, "Don't go deeper. Go back up. Don't let go!" Assuring myself over and over again that if I am crazy, I can't be aware of it, I manage to calm myself. But the doubts have found fertile ground.

Waking that morning I telephone Dr. van Zeale. I am in a real state by the time I'm put through to him. "I don't know if it is the pills or if I'm really going crazy," I cry agitatedly into the telephone, "but everything is chasing around in circles inside my head like it did before. All my ugly feelings have returned. I don't know what to do."

"You don't have to do anything, Mrs. Bielovich," he says calmly, smoothly. "Just continue with the pills and give them time to work."

"I don't have time to wait and see if they will work. I need help *now*! Right now! Don't you understand how desperate I am?" I scream.

His retort is unequivocal, "If you don't continue with the pills, I will have to recommit you."

Anxiety and nausea grip me as I slam down the phone. I can't bear the thought of returning to that dictatorship, or of losing my newly found freedom. And it isn't only my freedom I stand to lose in the equation—it's everyone and everything I know and that matters in my life. I feel very frightened.

Yet somewhere, deep down inside of me, there is a ray of hope, because as the day unfolds some of my unanswered questions begin to be resolved. I'm beginning to realize that Jack, my ex-convict friend, had been right all along. My real problems only started *after* I had been prescribed tranquillizers, antidepressants and sleeping pills. Up till then I had always coped and been in control, despite physical pain, despite operations, despite human tragedies, despite everything. Is it possible that the drugs have caused me to lose my mind? Is this the cause of my depression and illness? It seems to make sense. The more I think about it the more I am convinced that I have found the answer. But who will believe me, a patient from a mental institution?

Cautiously I raise this point with the Croatian priest, and he becomes quite heated. "Do you think you know more about medicine than the doctor? Do you want to go back there? If you do, you'd better understand I won't be coming to see you again," he says.

The following day, still hoping for some sort of solution. I mention my erratic feelings and concern to my daughter, Elizabeth. "Mommy, it's your life, your decision," she says. "Remember what I said to you before? We may not be around the next time." I feel sick and scared. There can never be a next time.

I realize the Catch-22 situation I am in. If I continue with the medication, my personality and behaviour will continue to deteriorate and the psychiatrist will eventually re-admit me. If I refuse to take the medication, the psychiatrist won't hesitate to recommit me, and I might be abandoned by an irate husband and family who would all consider me stubborn and insubordinate.

After much soul-searching, I conclude that there is only one avenue left open to me, the third option—that of lies and deceit. This is alien to my nature, but it's my only choice. Lies and deceit will have to be my travelling companions on this most hazardous part of my journey towards rehabilitation.

I have no doubt I am making the right choice, yet I'm fully aware that there will be a price to pay. It's a price I'm certainly prepared to pay if it means retaining both membership within my family and my sanity, so I agree to continue taking the pills on the condition my husband stop treating me like a child, watching me swallow them.

Believing I am sincere in my wish to get better, he relinquishes the absolute authority given him by Dr. van Zeale. But to my horror Nicky admonishes our daughters to keep their eyes open while I take the pills in front of them. So instead of one watch-dog, I now have a whole litter.

With the same guile, I appeal to the lot of them to stop treating me like a child. I give them my word that I will behave responsibly and, believing I am to be trusted, they hand the morning dose over to me, compounding the interest already growing in my deceit account. Evening time is trickier, as the pills and water are given a place of honour next to my husband's wine glass. Religiously I take them in front of everyone, place them under my tongue, then surreptitiously remove them when I go to the kitchen to bring something from the warmer, oven or fridge. It's remarkably easy, actually, and I settle uncomfortably into my double-life without raising anyone's suspicion.

And yet, as before, coming off the lithium and the newly prescribed drugs without any slow reduction in their dosage sends me on an unexpected ride through the house of horrors. I plunge down into nothingness one minute, surge upwards into outer space the next. I feel like a bunjee jumper let loose in the upper atmosphere. All my absolutes fall away and I no longer know who I am or where I am going. I no longer trust myself or my judgment. I feel lost in no man's land. The only thread linking me precariously to reality is attending daily Mass. I tell the family I am going out of gratitude, whereas in fact I am going in desperation, praying for the grace to get through the day without resorting to drugs.

Ironically, as the attacks grow further apart, the frightening symptoms seem to intensify. There are times when I feel my head is cracking down its centre, and I am paralysed with fear. Burrowing into my past, which I had earlier so ruthlessly tried to destroy, I search for a way to re-establish a connection with the person I had once been, reaffirming to myself, "I am Felicity, I am Felicity." Somehow I know it is vitally important that I hang onto her. If I don't, I will be lost forever.

There are many times I desperately want to share the truth with my family, but seeing how happy and carefree they are, having me at home, I can't bring myself to do it. On days when I really dare to *look* at them, I wonder how they possibly coped with the trauma of having a mother in a mental institution. When they enquire how I am feeling, trapped in my own deceit I must reply, "Just fine." Having endured enough pain, they are happy to accept and believe my lie.

Suffering from drug rebound and not knowing day by day how I will be, I grudgingly accept Cathy's invitation to join her nursery school class on a trip to "S.A.N.T.A.'s Mini-Town.*" Travelling in the bus, listening to the little ones singing, I know I am physically

* South African National Tuberculosis Association

present, but at the same time the immediate experience is not part of my reality. I'm here and I'm not here. My physical and mental states are disjointed, separated, and no amount of trying to draw them together seems to work. I am fragmented, parts all over, pieces missing. Throughout the day I feel this way, bewildered and confused, but somehow I make it through.

The stigma of having been in a mental institution hangs like a pall over everything I do as I struggle to regain my independence and self-confidence. Seeing an article in the newspaper about two young women who have started a business in their garage and enjoyed great success, I decide to join their organization, Home Executive Women (HEWS). When I meet them they are warm-hearted, generous and undemanding, and, following their lead, I begin to do needlework, fiddly things. I gradually build up stock, humble stock. I'm not over-ambitious. All I want is to break the ice, get back on the wheel of life.

To give myself credibility I have "Little Charmers" cards printed, and nervously tote my lacey little baskets to a prominent sweet shop in the city. They delightedly take them all, order more, and put me in touch with an exclusive suburban shop. When I deliver the order to the owner, a fatherly, chatty Continental, my confidence is again boosted when he turns my product over in his hand and comments, "I can see a great deal of love has gone into this. I'll take them all."

My husband still accompanies me monthly to see Dr. van Zeale, where they continue to discuss me and my now seemingly formidable progress. I never interrupt during these sessions. Nor do I mention my raging inner struggle. On my fourth visit, however, there is a nasty surprise waiting for me at the end of their usual consultation. Dr. van Zeale, believing my progress is due to the tablets, announces that he wants blood tests done within the fortnight; that way he can monitor my medication and reduce my visits to once a quarter.

Nicky is absolutely delighted at this wonderful news and afterwards takes me out for dinner. I try to be gracious, but realize with a sinking heart that my time has run out.

Fear eats at my innards as I contemplate the reaction and consequences when family and doctor discover the truth. I hurry to my pharmacist, pour out my heart to him about the forthcoming blood tests and ask his advice. "Listen Felicity, you've coped fantastically," he says. "When I think of all the pills you've swallowed over the last eighteen months, and how you've managed to stay off them, I think you're wonderful. It's time the family and the psychiatrist heard the truth and learned just how well you've managed." I ask him what the psychiatrist is likely to say, and he jokingly replies, "He's probably going to kill you." But then adds more reassuringly, "There's really nothing he can do."

I hope he is right. But the fourteen days leading to the blood tests are the longest in my life. I have to appear absolutely normal, hide my inner turmoil until my due date arrives, then I can finally break with my recent past and deliver the truth. The incongruity of the situation is almost too much for me when we share a family meal with the Croatian priest one evening, and he says how wonderful it is to see us together again, a happy and united family once more, and how proud he is of me for listening to reason and taking the medication. I almost fall off my chair.

Inevitably, the day arrives. I am extremely nervous, but hype myself up by telling myself how great I am for giving up the pills on my own. I select my clothes with great care—a chic black suit and white silk blouse. I pin a beautiful cultured pearl brooch, an anniversary gift from Nicky, on the lapel for good luck. As we are leaving, I tell myself for about the hundredth time I am ready.

We are sitting in the doctor's consulting room. As usual, my husband is giving the gospel of Felicity, and the doctor is totally entranced by all I've accomplished. I am too. I have indeed come a long, long way. At the end of the good news, Dr. van Zeale buzzes for the nurse to come and draw my blood. I have rehearsed this moment many, many times in my mind, but when the sister looms in the doorway, syringe in hand, I freeze for one panic-stricken moment, then finding my courage blurt out, "Blood tests are unnecessary. I never took the pills. I got better on my own."

Dr. van Zeale raises his eyebrows in surprise, then frowns deeply, his nose starting to twitch. Scrummaging in my handbag I repeat even louder, "I got better on my own, my own. Do you understand?"

The doctor's face clouds over, as he struggles to comprehend what I have just said. But before he can open his mouth I empty out all my colourless, saliva-worn tablets across his much-doodled blotter. Both men are totally dumbstruck, disbelief stamped on carbon-copy faces. Nicky is the first to recover. He feels betrayed at my deceit and can only repeat, "You gave us your word, you promised us, we trusted you. Why didn't you tell *me*?"

Dr. van Zeale, still gathering his wits, springs from his swivel chair and bumps his thigh on the corner of the desk. A raw expletive explodes from his trembling lips before he comes to a halt where I am seated. "You can't make a bloody fool of me like this and get away with it, do you hear? I'll send you back; you're still committed!" The sister, still standing in the doorway, syringe in hand, is oblivious to the scene being played out and asks blithely, "Must I take the blood now, Doctor?" I yell over all their voices, "Phone the professor! He'll tell how well I've coped on my own. Go on, phone him. Phone him NOW!" Dr. van Zeale refuses and an ugly scene ensues as my spleen erupts like a volcano, emitting a gaseous, oozing lava of suppressed anger, humiliation, frustration and self-imposed guilt. While he tries to regain his authority and composure I, now calmed by my catharsis, make a grand picadorlike exit, thrusting the final dart by saying, "I'll see you in court!" What court I have no idea, but it's wonderfully exhilarating having the last word.

Outside on the pavement, I dance around hugging myself, repeating over and over again, "Yes, yes! Yes—I did it!" I'm certain I'm over the final barrier. I feel alive, rejuvenated, free. I feel unafraid and strong. I want to shout and grab every passer-by telling them I have just won the greatest victory of my life. I feel restored, reintegrated. Each time I picture the doctor's shocked and angry face I burst out laughing. When Nicky finally emerges from the clinic he still looks upset, but he's not angry.

Driving home in the car we laugh like children, the first time in eighteen months that we have both felt unrestrained and natural, able to share from our hearts. We arrive home and tell the girls what transpired in the consulting room, and they all laugh as well. There are no recriminations; all agree that in this case the end justified the means. I am home to stay. I'm sure I'm over the final hurdle.

CHAPTER FIVE

The Heart Is Sane

I am not of course over the final hurdle. The very next day I am wondering how I could ever have been so naïve as to think that having everything out in the open would make the ambiguity disappear. It has only made matters worse. Having pretended now for three months that I was reintegrated, how can I now suddenly say to everyone that my mind still seems to be detached from my body? That my moods are still extremely erratic? That I parachute up and down like a yo-yo? If I do they'll be justifiably angry that I hadn't taken the medication, even more justified in believing that I am indeed mentally unstable. I realize that I am now totally on my own, that I am solely responsible for my actions. There can be no looking back. I feel completely isolated, but I continue to reassure myself, *I am Felicity. I am. I am.*

Over the next few weeks I realize it is a prejudiced and judgmental world I'm returning to. I've been in a madhouse, gone off my rocker, lost my marbles, flown over the cuckoo's nest, and so I'm forever tainted. Everyone has their own interpretation, theory and reason for my being put *inside,* but it would be easier if I was labelled a thief or murderer because then at least my crime would make fewer people uneasy or confused. Because my illness has failed to meet the criteria for external cause or manifest symptoms which everyone can recognize—bloodied bandages, a plaster cast, multiple drips, gallstones in a jar—I must endure the stigma associated with mental illness.

Stigma is not something you can easily see or touch. It is much more subtle than that. It is something which is *felt* at the core of one's being, an invisible barrier which cuts, separates, alienates, makes you feel that you are different, not quite right, a misfit. And it isn't reserved solely for mental patients either. Society determines who its social outcasts are and their degree of separateness and even the guilt they should feel, and it does so from a broad palette.

I am soon acutely aware that the Institution has sent me out to rehabilitate myself without any counselling or preparation for the preconceptions and ignorance they must have known I would meet. I have still not been given any explanation as to *why* I was committed in the first place, and I do not feel equipped to defend myself or deal with the smug replies of those it-would-never-happen-to-me people who, by way of innuendo or condescending attitude, make me feel ashamed of myself. I feel emotionally naked, alone and in limbo. Maybe I'm not really better. Maybe I'm a fraud. Maybe I really do belong back at the Institution. These thoughts haunt me as I try to put my fragile life back together.

Each day presents a new set of obstacles. Each time I think I am getting myself together, some reminder, subtle or otherwise, surfaces, and my self-worth plummets. At a kitchen tea one afternoon, with a varied group of friends and family members present, the subject of depression arises. Suzanne, an erstwhile friend, shares, in great detail, how I'd looked and behaved when I had been depressed. She holds everyone captive by telling them, "You should have seen her face and eyes. They looked awful." She elaborates animatedly, obviously enjoying her dissertation. "She was wearing this old dress with the hem half hanging out. I could see she had no pride left, because it didn't worry her. Of course, I couldn't bring myself to tell her what she looked like."

"No, she couldn't. But she's now having no difficulty telling everybody else," I think.

Suzanne carries on in an authoritative tone about what she has recently read concerning the lurid consequences of shock treatment. In doing so she manages to reopen a raw wound in my psyche. She seems to relish saying that people who have shock treatment end up mad. Would we like to see the copy of the magazine and the pictures? "What if she tells everybody *I've* been inside?" I think to myself, becoming increasingly agitated. I want to leave the room, but I'm scared to in case she does tell them. Continuing her story, Suzanne offers her own theory as to who becomes depressed—women who stay at home, people who are spoilt, bored, have nothing to show for their lives, and particularly mothers whose children are leaving home. This last point is made while looking directly into my eyes.

"I don't think any of those reasons apply to me Suzanne," I say in a quavering voice, rising to my own defence. "I think my problem may have something to do with the pills I took."

"Yes, but you just took them and look where you landed," Suzanne says, not letting it go. I nod my head knowingly. Then, before she can tell everybody exactly where that was, I blurt out, "Five months in hospital and a mental institution." Everybody is dumbstruck. My daughters give me the thumbs-up sign. My heart is pounding.

Suzanne jumps up. "Let's go inside for tea," she says tartly. We do, and the topic does not arise again, but I feel myself ridden by guilt and shame.

A few days later I am walking around the garden on a fresh Sunday afternoon, looking for the early signs of spring on the trees and shrubs, when friends arrive. One of them approaches me and asks what I am doing. Before I can reply she reminds me, "You know what happens to people who do nothing." With eyebrows raised pointedly she adds, "You must keep yourself occupied." I have always kept myself busy, but now, I realize with a shock, I will have to be *seen* to be doing something at all times.

Drawing up the guest list for Cathy's wedding the next evening, the dreadful, familiar words, "Don't go, don't go"—those same words which had nearly ruined Cathy's graduation day—re-echo in my mind. Oh God, am I crazy after all?

Too ashamed to visit our new parish priest, I hurry off to a priest in Johannesburg to discuss my fears. Arriving in record time outside a beautifully carved presbytery door, I ring the bell for long minutes until it is finally opened by an ascetic, fatherly looking man with kind eyes. Before he can even say good morning I blurt out, "I am *possessed*!" He leads me into a well-lit and tidy office where I give him a garbled account of the previous months' agony. Then I break down into tears, shamefully telling him I don't want to attend my own daughter's wedding.

He is everything a priest should be—compassionate, empathetic, discerning, nonjudgmental. Above all he is a sensitive listener. His approach is direct and practical; his counsel sound and absolutely honest. Speaking quietly, he tells me not to be afraid, I am definitely not possessed. He explains that I am experiencing "flashbacks" from an obviously traumatic and intense experience. He takes me into the church and prays over me, asking me to trust in God a little longer. A marvellous feeling of tranquillity comes over me and I return home.

I am now leading a much fuller and more active life, but I am still a long way from being fully integrated. I feel like a complicated thousand-piece puzzle—the frame is nearing completion, but there are still numerous pieces remaining to complete the picture. Hoping that my life will finally gel, I diligently continue with Cathy's wedding arrangements. Sitting in a group with all the girls one afternoon, listening to them talking about Cathy's house and future, I realize they all have purpose, vision, direction. I feel like a displaced person, travelling without a map or destination. Whereas I had always advised them and others on what to do to get their lives together, now it is me in search of a framework. I try to draw hope from the small things I *have* achieved since returning home.

The great day is approaching but I feel as if I am on parole. Negative statements from various people—"I wonder how she's going to cope on the day? Do you think she can handle Cathy leaving home?"—come back to me. Though nervous and scared, I feel I *am* coping. I wish I had the courage and confidence to turn to everyone and say, "Listen here, it's quite normal to be anxious for your first child's wedding." But I can't say that because my system is still in the process of rebalancing itself, and every bit of self-doubt will be suspect.

Yet, somehow, with the grace of God and much hard work on my part, everything comes together beautifully as the wedding day arrives. We all rise early and have an emotional breakfast, as Cathy is showered with little keepsakes from all of us. The wedding party goes off to get their hair done, while I collect the bouquets and corsages. I excitedly tell the florist all the little details as she places the flowers in boxes. Caught up in wedding fever now, I visit the church, admire the beautiful floral arrangements on the altar, and silently thank God for them, this day and the shafts of warm sunlight penetrating the stained-glass windows.

On my way home I decide the car should be cleaned and drive up to the garage nearest our house. Then it happens. Whether it is a build-up of excitement, jangled nerves or lack of spatial perception I don't know, but instead of entering the washing cubicle, I hit the little thatch hut alongside. I jump out of the car and see half the length of the chrome-stripped bumper almost touching the ground. I try to lift it and it falls off, along with the number plate. I dash into the garage, see the owner and frantically tell him it is the bride's car, and this her wedding day! He has to do something, anything! This is not a BMW garage, however, and he doesn't carry spare parts. Nevertheless, seeing how distraught I am, he has a plan. An hour later I drive away from the garage with a bumper that no one would know is in fact held together with little more than a prayer and a young mechanic's ingenuity.

I head home shaken to the core. Had it just been wedding jitters or is it something more sinister? I don't have time to find out, because when I arrive everyone is rushing madly in all directions. I join the mêlée in the bedroom. While I am putting the final touches to Cathy's veil, the photographer and Nicky join us for the procession out of the house. It's raining and everyone is quickly bundled into the waiting cars.

I battle to hold back tears of joy and gratitude as I watch Cathy walk down the aisle on her proud father's arm. As we settle into the nuptial Mass, I remember the damaged bumper, and my mind flees down the corridor of doubt and fear. Am I forever going to look back? Surely on this special day God will grant me peace of mind?

Leaving a confetti trail behind us we move off to a beautiful garden for the traditional family photographs. Cathy expresses her wish for a last picture with "Mommy and Daddy." I link arms with her and face the camera, Cathy turns to me and says, "I love you very, very much, Mom. Thank you for being *my* mom." My heart is full to bursting.

Awakening the next day, looking back on the see-saw of emotions I experienced during the wedding, I realize for the first time that they are only the tip of a huge iceberg of frozen feelings, feelings which have been anaesthetized by the pills. And I also realize that if I try to awaken these feelings too hastily, anything might happen. Somehow my heart will have to resolve these feelings in its own time. Inevitably this will involve emotional pain. Christmas opens my heart to the first seepage.

I find the carols by candlelight, the lit-up Christmas trees, the gift-laden shoppers, the shining, expectant faces of the children almost too painful to bear. They all remind me of what my family missed the previous year. I feel guilty, ashamed, full of regrets, and so go wildly overboard in my own Christmas shopping. As I watch my husband and daughters open their extravagant gifts after midnight Mass I can't help wondering whether their joy is superficial; whether they, like me, continually look back in sorrow. I am too heartsore to ask.

It's an agonizing Christmas for me, but I do gain two important insights. My overboard shopping crystallizes for me how deeply I have buried the painful past; how I am in fact trying to create a kind of emotional amnesia. My instincts tell me this is wrong. A monstrous event has occurred in my life; my mind had been ripped open like a house in a tornado. There is no point trying to deny that fact, or ignore its consequences.

The second thing I discern is that I have been left to clear up the aftermath of the tornado with little or no outside resources. I don't know whether to build upon old foundations or start from scratch; what to salvage, what to discard. I alone have to put my life back together working with no personal expertise and very few guidelines. It is a daunting realization.

At New Year's I make a comprehensive list of noble resolutions. I will look only forward, face the future, seek the whole, uphold the good, make wise choices, set achievable goals, bear responsibility for my actions, manage time effectively, harness my energy and exercise tremendous self-discipline. Within days I realize how totally unrealistic I've been in thinking I can achieve all this. No one could, and my mind keeps returning to the past. This is going to be far more difficult than I thought.

One night I ask Nicky what sort of person he thinks I am or was. "How have you coped and felt during my absence?" I ask, genuinely needing to know. He sits back quietly, watching me thoughtfully, deciding what to tell me. Weighing his words carefully, he finally tells me how he shared numerous evenings with our daughters sitting around the table into the early hours of the morning, trying to reassure them that everything was going to turn out fine. He tells me of his own doubts and fears, and how he never fully understood what was happening to me. I feel his pain and suffering. He relates an incident when Debby, our youngest daughter, came home from school devastated because her friends had found out where I was. My heart aches for her. I realize how much they have all matured and grown within themselves, how they have all drawn strength from each other and drawn closer together. No wonder they are so closely knit.

Unaware of the impact his words are having on me, Nicky carries on, telling me of offers he has received from women, in my absence, over the counter at the butchery—weekends at the cottage, tickets to the theatre. Others were far more blatant in their appeal, "Your wife's not coming back, Nicky. My bed is yours."

Lying in bed that night I am plagued with self-blame and the nightmarish thought that I could have lost my husband. My emotions churn around like a blender. And yet, despite the cavorting demons, some part of me knows that this is a positive and necessary step. Perhaps for the first time since my release, I am directly in touch with my wounded heart.

The heart is life's barometer; it's central to our well-being, and I know my task is to somehow heal my wounded heart. I know, too, that I must learn to listen to the heart's vital language, to trust it, to allow it to inform me when I am loved, wanted, needed—or mistreated. The heart can be abused in a number of ways—by inconsiderate people, unpredictable events, the spoken or unspoken word. If someone or something injures the heart, it can become cold, hard, mean, shrivelled. If ignored, it demands full compensation.

In my case my heart has spoken, only I don't know its language. I can't comprehend what my heart is so desperately trying to tell me. But this insight makes it abundantly clear to me how much self-blame, guilt, deep-seated anger and other unfinished business I still have to attend to before I can be fully reconciled to myself. As yet, I don't know how this will come about.

I realize that nearly six months of my life has been completely wiped out, lost, taken. Unfortunately, I can't buy back any of the time I have lost, nor can I save some for a rainy day. I have to spend the time I now have wisely. Today. Now. But I still have a tangle of loose threads to sort out before this is possible. With this new awareness, I finally fall asleep, and awaken in the morning feeling stronger.

Our silver anniversary approaches, and I find it more difficult than ever to avoid dwelling upon past events. I feel like someone recently bereaved, always recalling where I had been, what I had been doing a year earlier. The anniversary is celebrated by having Mass said in our house, during which Nicky and I renew our wedding vows. Nicky has more than honoured his, and I feel deeply in his debt. My heart is overflowing but, looking around at the girls, I can't help thinking of the interwoven feelings they must hold in the secret chambers of their hearts. I realize I am seeing what the neurologist, psychiatrist, health professional seldom sees—the devastating and far-reaching effect my breakdown had on each member of my family. Having lived in the eye of the storm, they too are its victims. My countless sojourns to the hospital for physical maladies never wreaked the havoc and upheaval that five months spent in a psychological mincing-machine has done. The fact that they have come through the experience whole and healthy only bears testimony to their inner strength and character.

For our anniversary, Nicky spoils me with two strings of magnificent pearls. I am enraptured with them, and, curious about their origin, ask him for the name of the agent. After arranging an appointment, I meet Ingrid, a beautiful young lady, at the pearl's wholesaler, and we chat easily. Much to my surprise, she asks me if I would be interested in selling the pearls. I'm hesitant to embark upon such a venture, but she suggests I make a study of pearls and sit the Jewellery Council exam. She and her directors show such great confidence in me that I do so, and thus soon found myself supplied with a ransomable amount of pearls and a new mini-career.

It is a tremendous learning experience and adventure for me, both professionally and personally. Not only do I learn to calculate tax, keep books and manage stock, but I also encounter a broad spectrum of people who provide me with "pearls" of a significantly different nature. As only someone who has sold pearls could know, many of the men and women to whom I sell pearls have their own particular story to tell as to why they want to possess this queen of gems. Every string of pearls I sell is wrapped in a history of previously unknown intimacy for the delighted recipient, and, like a priest, I become privy to many secrets and intimate stories linking whole networks of friends. Hearing these secrets, however, like the oyster my lips remain sealed. They also remain sealed whenever it comes to admitting to anyone that I am still trying to put my own fragmented life back together. I wonder if I will ever have the courage to admit that I had once been drug-dependent, contemplated suicide, been committed to a psychiatric/mental institution and come out the other side.

Sometimes my clients mention that they are experiencing difficulties with their drug-taking spouse or child, describing irrational behaviour and changing moods, and my stomach twists into a knot. It's like listening to my own story told by a stranger. These disturbing accounts often lead to flashbacks as a web of lost memories resurfaces at odd intervals. I know these memories could become very destructive, but I try to use them as one would a torch, to light up hidden recesses and gain new insights. Despite my growth and relative surface calm, I'm aware there are still dangerous emotional undercurrents in my psyche that remain unresolved.

I am at a house party one morning demonstrating the versatility of pearls to a small group of ladies when an elegant lady of uncertain age compliments me on my knowledge of pearls, as well as on my "superlative" delivery. "I can see you're a very experienced and trained speaker," she adds. I nod graciously, not bothering to correct her erroneous assessment of me, and when she continues with an invitation to address her "group" I am only too glad to agree, thoroughly puffed up with myself as I am by then. I ask the address of her house, where I assume the presentation will take place, and I'm sure everyone in the room can hear my ego audibly deflating when she replies, "Oh not at my house, my dee-ah, at the club." I manage to suppress the rising tide of panic, keep a smile plastered inanely to my face and nod as she fills in further the details of the coming event—the club she is referring to is one of the most prestigious in the area, and there will be three hundred "membahs" in attendance! I've never addressed more than twenty people at one time! I flee in terror toward Ingrid, hoping she will calm my panic. Instead she bursts out laughing.

Ingrid is, however, marvellously supportive in the coming days, and these are spent in a flurry of arranging for models, selecting dresses, and rehearsing my address over and over again. The night prior to the event is spent tossing, turning, pleading and praying. At the event itself, as I sit waiting for my introduction, I am fitted with a lapel microphone, only adding to my consternation. Unaware that the microphone has already been switched on, as I stand to approach the podium I lean toward Ingrid and whisper, "I'll talk, you pray." Everyone in the auditorium hears me; they all laugh, and it is a superb icebreaker. My presentation is a tremendous success.

Driving home from the presentation, my buoyant spirits in step with the Tritsch-Tratsch Polka playing on the radio, I realize I have taken a giant step forward, not for mankind, but for myself. My happy thoughts are interrupted, however, by an announcement from the radio that, after the commercial break, an eminent professor will be discussing "the use and abuse of minor tranquillizers" with a panel of experts. This I must listen to. Taking the next off-ramp, I park under a huge oak tree in a quiet neighbourhood and adjust the volume on the radio.

Briefly the professor explains that minor tranquillizers, or "benzodiazepines," are depressants of the central nervous system, and that overenthusiastic prescribing of them can lead to tolerance and dependence. In some cases, explains the professor, prolonged ingestion of tranquillizers can in fact aggravate depressive illness and provoke suicide. He also talks about how tranquillizers are eliminated very slowly from the body, how they may accumulate in specific "binding sites" of the brain, and how this in turn means that various undesirable side-effects can persist long after a patient has stopped taking the drug. There is consensus among the panel members on the value of tranquillizers as a premedication before surgery, or for a few days' use in situations of acute anxiety or crisis, but when it comes to regular use for more than a week or two the discussion becomes heated. I find their arguments perplexing at times but they hold my interest—enormously.

As the professor continues to expound upon the adverse side-effects of tranquillizers, to my astonishment, I find I can verify every word he is uttering. In fact, as he and the other panel members describe the various symptoms, I realize I am at that moment reliving them. The sleeping libido, memory impairment, the self-destructive urges, sporadic awareness of actual events, depersonalization, rebound anxiety and insomnia, all are familiar to me. As I sit in my car listening, I find I am back down the dark passage looking for an escape from the turbulent, disturbing thoughts and questions raging in my now thoroughly confused mind. If tranquillizers have such a history of negative side-effects why are they being so freely prescribed? Is it because the doctors lack the necessary time? Is it simply a case of hurriedly treating the crying and agitated, the nonsleepers and the can't-get-ups with the easiest available means? Or is it a case of patients abusing their doctors, demanding prescriptions to overcome personal problems, knowing that if their doctor doesn't co-operate they can simply march off to another doctor who will comply with their demand? Is it a matter of poor communication on both sides? Have we as a society become so quick to turn to pills as a solution that these pills now dictate, determine, dominate, drive our lives?

The authoritative voice of the professor describing "the limbic system" snaps me out of my ongoing confusion. I remember how George, Elizabeth's fiancé, had tried to explain this physiology to me when I had felt so desperate. It is fascinating to learn that the limbic system is the emotional centre of the brain, that it signals reward and punishment. Is this why I continually blame and punish myself for my uncharacteristic behaviour? Mind darting, thoughts connecting, realization dawning, I am so disturbed I have to force myself to listen further.

The broadcast over, I drive hurriedly off to visit my pharmacist. I want accurate information on all the drugs I'd been prescribed, and I want it now. At the pharmacy, reading the contra-indications on the data sheets, I become increasingly alarmed. Many of the indications apply directly to me at the time of taking the drugs. When my eyes fall on the word "depression" listed as a side-effect for several of the pills, fierce anger and a devastating sense of betrayal nearly overwhelm me. My neurologist had not only prescribed these pills religiously for a long time, but he had also neglected to allow a reasonable break between cessation of the former drug, and trying a new one, as the professor on the radio had stated one should do. I seethe with anger.

My first reaction is litigation. I will haul the neurologist before a board of enquiry, sue, see him forever expelled from his profession! But I know that doctors everywhere have a reputation for closing ranks whenever a peer is challenged by a patient. Undeterred, I let my imagination run wild with a hundred alternatives. I want to punch his aquiline nose to a pulp, watch his blood trickle down onto his pristine shirt and Christian Dior tie. I want to thrust a handful of "try these" tablets down his enlarged Adam's apple, lock him up in a Judas room. Perhaps a few of his colleagues should accompany him so they too can have a taste of what it's like to be a victim of betrayal, to feel the loss of one's liberty, rights, pride, persona, without any guarantee of ever having any of it restored. That has a ring of justice to it. I give the matter deep thought before deciding what I will do. His humiliation has to be public—in his artfully designed and always overcrowded waiting-room.

I set out that Friday afternoon still thirsting for blood, anger and revenge raging in my heart. I arrive at the clinic in a volcanic mood. Ignoring the lift, I march determinedly up the stairs. Striding through the open door into the waiting-room I find it is exactly as I had anticipated—overcrowded. A young child resting quietly on her mother's lap looks up at me inquiringly, while other patients raise their eyes from their magazines in polite curiosity. In that brief moment, with all their eyes upon me, I know I don't have the moral justification to carry out my intended course of action. To them, he may be a wonderful neurologist, a miracle man, an answer to their prayers. I can't be responsible for destroying their faith, belief and, above all, their hope.

The receptionist is already paging through her appointment book, trying to place my face to a name. I look around for a moment, then turn, saying nothing, and leave the room. Going down in the lift, I know I've done the right thing. Ten minutes on centre stage screaming abuse is certainly very tempting, but it would have given only a modicum of the satisfaction I need. And afterwards I would, no doubt, have simply been dismissed as irrational, even crazy. But anger like mine, so deeply rooted in the psyche, doesn't just disappear because it's been suppressed. At some point it has to be spent, whether in small outbursts or a singular eruption. Somehow I have to find a more constructive outlet for my outrage, one which will prevent others from following in my footsteps.

After much thought, I decide to harness my anger in a tool, a writing tool. By telling my story, perhaps I can create a new degree of awareness and alert ordinary people to the dangers of passively accepting prescriptions without first questioning the diagnosis or prognosis. I can inform them that by exercising their rights as patients they empower themselves to have a say in their own health care.

But before I can tell my story I will first have to heal myself completely, deal with the toxic waste still remaining from the whole experience. A host of very real feelings—resentment, anger, guilt, self-blame—still reside in my core and they have to be disposed of. I feel strong enough to commence, and so I set out on an inner journey, praying that somewhere along the road my head and heart will fuse. I make a pact with myself to be nonjudgmental, uncritical and truthful in my quest.

Like an archaeologist, I tunnel down into the hallowed ground of my own psyche. I proceed with great trepidation, aware that I have no training in such an undertaking, and I tread softly, very softly, as I set out first of all to unearth my suppressed feelings. Working my way back through events in time I quickly discover huge chunks of unresolved anger and self-hatred, and these at first stop me cold, make me want to flee. But I persevere, and discover that, with time and persistence, I can break up these chunks of foul emotions into manageable pieces. It is a revelation to me how my past humiliations, misjudgments and mistakes, acts of omission and commission, can be robbed of their frightening power if I see them in the light of my own human frailty. I also learn to see these skeletons as what they are—worthless and useless. No one could possibly regret ridding themselves of them.

The overall pace of my inner journey remains slow, however, and my improvement continues to be characterized by periods of joyous progress, followed by times of anxious self-doubt. Guilt—"Why didn't I. . . ? If only I had. . . ."—is probably the most sinister and persistent of the various feelings lurking within my wounded heart, the sort of guilt that could drive one to recontemplate suicide. Because of the compassion and understanding I have received from Nicky and the girls, I've never become suicidal again, but, because of the guilt imposed by both myself and others, the wound continues to fester.

Despite this, as I continue my journey towards integration, the root of self-acceptance establishes itself in my heart and before long I begin to experience the sweet taste of self-forgiveness. In forgiving myself I forgive the neurologist, and feel the lifting of an immense burden. As I let go of other negatives binding me to my past I begin to feel joy. My heart begins to open, and like that first morning at home after returning from the institution, I realize again that I own myself, and this self-ownership gives me a wonderful sense of security, well-being and mastery over my own personal domain. Knowing that no one can rob me of this mastery, unless I give them the permission to do so, empowers and convinces me at last that I have the ability to determine my own fate.

I am a very different Felicity the day I pay a return visit to the Institution. When I park outside the entrance and look up the long winding drive, I can't help feeling sorrow for all the others who are still suffering as I had suffered. My visit crystallizes for me just how much my own recovery had been supported by the love and comfort provided by my husband and daughters. Without them I might still be within those walls. But what of all those stricken people within who have no such family support? What happens to them? Theirs indeed must be a lonely and painful road to recovery.

And what of those family members who do try to support their ailing loved ones, but who often do not know how to even express what is happening to them while recovery is taking place. These family members suffer too. Mostly they tread very gently, holding their breath in fear of what might happen. Often they live on a see-saw—happiness and hope on one side, fear and doubt on the other. They're happy to see recovery in progress, but fearful that it may not last. And this doubt makes them skirt the possibility of asking questions, expressing their feelings or making suggestions—inaction which is to everyone's detriment.

I know this had certainly been true in my case. My daughters were constantly wondering if I would ever come home; once I did they were wondering if my return was permanent, or whether they would have to face another painful "episode." They were too scared to articulate this fear, so they suppressed their feelings in an unhealthy crippling silence. A great deal of their suffering could have been avoided if even one of the health care professionals involved in my case had taken the time to explain the recovery process to them. In failing to do so, my daughters were deprived of a vital lifeline. These people left my daughters to find their way on their own.

As I gaze at the Institution, I well understand why the girls had felt such fear of and aversion to the place. Yet within myself I find no horror or recrimination, only peace. At this moment I feel the presence of God, and the full impact of my recovery strikes home. An air of reconciliation rises thick around me, and I feel my spirit becoming lighter and stronger. I feel my heart opening as sorrows, joys, darkness and light stream out. I see now what has been hidden from me for too long. The ultimate pearl is mine for the taking. All I need to do is acknowledge the gifts of my life, the many things I have been blessed with, the thousand ways in which I am so fortunate. I am back, back with my family, back on my own path, unimpeded and content. The past is the past but I, Felicity, will create the future. This I know for I, Felicity, am finally whole again. I, Felicity, am healed.

POSTSCRIPT

In the end the Croatian priest was right. My bitter experience was and still is a source of personal growth and spiritual enrichment for me. Out of my experience I wrote my first book, *Beyond the Barrier*, which I then forwarded to psychiatrists, doctors and health groups both at home and abroad. In response I have received enormous feedback regarding the dangers of benzodiazepines, or minor tranquillizers. (Minor tranquillizers are to be distinguished from the major tranquillizers which are used extensively in the pharmacological treatment of schizophrenia.) I now have a significant store of resource data—a source of knowledge I can only wish I possessed at the time of my institutionalization. I have shared this information with numerous groups, including a high-profile mental health conference, and I currently run an educational programme on coping with anxiety, depression and stress without resorting to pharmaceutical means.

The history of benzodiazepines begins with approval by the American Food and Drug Administration of Librium in 1960. Three years later Valium was first marketed in the U.S. and in 1965 Mogodon was introduced. Since then there have been a veritable plethora of such drugs marketed under a bewildering series of chemical and brand names, until, by 1979, it was estimated that there were about 700 Valium-like drugs on the market. By 1985, Dr. Vernon Coleman, writing in his book *Life Without Tranquillissers*, was able to state that: "The benzodiazepines are now almost certainly the most widely prescribed group of drugs in the world and the biggest selling drugs in the history of medicine."

The amount of money involved in the marketing of these drugs is nothing less than staggering. In 1994, in the United States alone, there were 60 million prescriptions dispensed in the category of "anxiolytics," (drugs to relieve anxiety) with sales exceeding $1.2 billion. Worldwide, it is estimated that in 1994 sales of "central nervous system pharmaceuticals" (a class of drugs somewhat wider than benzodiazepines but defined as any prescription drug used to treat mental disorders) totalled more than $21 billion U.S. Overall, when we include all types of drugs sold anywhere in the world, the *New York Times* has concluded that, as of 1996, the pharmaceutical industry has annual revenues of at least $200 billion U.S.

It's ironic to note that the minor tranquillizers were initially marketed as a much better alternative to barbiturates, a class of drugs which had become notorious for producing psychological and physical dependence, as well as untold lethal overdoses. What's more, as each new tranquillizer was introduced by the various drug companies, each was hailed as being better than its predecessors and free of any significant side-effects. "Ultran" was introduced by the Eli Lilly Company as the "ultimate tranquillizer," and ads promised that the drug "does not affect intellectual or motor abilities." When Merck Sharp and Dohme introduced "Suavitil" it too was said to "leave the quality of thinking virtually unchanged." Suavitil had "no hypnotic effect," although it would "relieve sleeplessness by reducing repetitive thinking (futile rumination)." Each of the new drugs was also of course "new." Ultran was "chemically unique," and Suavitil differed "fundamentally from any of the substances currently used in this field." When Librium was first marketed, the advertising catchphrase was all-inclusive—"Whatever the diagnosis . . . Librium." Quickly, however, as the list of new drugs grew, the drug companies began to stress that, more than being just "new," the different drugs were intended for distinct purposes—Tentone was a compound "for the lower and middle range of disorders," and Trancopal was introduced as a "tranquilaxant," that is both a muscle relaxant and tranquillizer. Atarax, the "passport to tranquillity," was claimed to be "antihistaminic, antiarrhythmic and antisecretory."

There is in fact very little difference among the various benzodiazepines. And in my case, as in countless others, the bogus differentiation among benzodiazepines led to serious problems. My doctor apparently failed to realize that different benzodiazepines belong to the same class of drugs, and therefore prescribed two or three at the same time, needlessly compounding the problems. Additionally, my doctor seemed not to understand that the effect of benzodiazepines is additive—two drugs at regular dosage have the same effect as either drug at double the regular dose. Again, both these problems are common. (I leave aside here the very significant and unnecessary financial cost to the public caused by the differentiation of benzodiazepines.) Part of this particular aspect of the problem can be explained by the fact that very often tranquillizers are prescribed by "primary care providers" rather than by qualified psychiatrists, that is doctors who are general practitioners without specialized knowledge of benzodiazepines and their side-effects. One recent study indicated, for instance, that as few as 15% of patients receiving benzodiazepines had seen a psychiatrist in the preceding year.

As time passed following the introduction of the first tranquillizers, it became readily apparent that, despite the claims of the drug companies, all of the various tranquillizers were capable of producing a frightening variety of side-effects—memory loss, the impairment of coordination, reduced sexual desire, at times even rage or hostility rather than the advertised tranquillity. Perhaps even more alarming though, was the clear emergence of the fact that all benzodiazepines, if taken long enough, produce psychological and physical dependence. It seems that, over time, the brain learns to expect a certain level of the drug, and if the drug is removed, the brain reacts with agitation, sleeplessness and anxiety—the very symptoms which often led the patient to begin taking the drug in the first place. Frequently these symptoms are worse than the original ones, a phenomenon known as the "rebound effect."

While conducting research I was intrigued to read a 1992 Australian report—"Be Wise with Medicines: A Federal Government Initiative"—that stated: "If used for longer than a few weeks the benzodiazepines may produce a range of symptoms, some of which can be severe. Many of these side-effects look and feel like symptoms of psychological disorder: agitation, extreme anxiety, depression, lethargy, agrophobia, irrational behaviour and mental confusion. These side-effects of the medication have often been understandably mistaken for a patient's mental state." Thus not only can tranquillizers produce side-effects more aggravated than the original symptoms, they can in fact *cause* a diagnosis of mental illness when no disorder was initially present.

The only genuine difference which does exist among the various tranquillizers relates to the drug's "half-life." The half-life of a drug defines how long, on average, it takes for half the amount of an ingested drug to be cleared from the body; the mid-point measurement is used because drugs are not cleared at an even rate. The half-life suggests how long the effects of a single dose are likely to persist and whether or not the drug will accumulate in the body. The shorter the half-life, the sooner one can expect withdrawal effects to appear, and the more severe they may be. One result of a shorter half-life is the increased likelihood of addiction, a factor well illustrated by the introduction of Xanax in 1981. Xanax was heralded as the first of a new class of tranquillizers with a very short half-life—drugs completely eliminated by the body in less than half a day. But this very fact exacerbates the withdrawal symptoms of benzodiazepine dependency. Whereas the longer half-life of a drug like Valium means a more gradual elimination of the drug, Xanax's very short half-life results in an acute withdrawal syndrome that can include cramps, twitching, impaired concentration and occasionally even seizures—a phenomenon much more likely to cause the patient to resume taking the drug. Despite this fact, in 1986 Xanax surpassed Valium as the most widely prescribed tranquillizer in the world. (1994 revenues for Xanax worldwide totalled $342 million U.S.)

The popularity of the benzodiazepines as prescription drugs is no mystery when one considers the amount of money the drug companies spend in promoting them, and the way in which they spend it. In Canada, for example, a 1996 radio report on the Canadian Broadcasting Corporation recounted that the drug companies spend roughly $10,000 *per doctor* in persuading them to dispense the desired pills. In the United States, the government's Food and Drug Administration was forced to crack down recently when the public became aware that the drug companies were sending doctors and their spouses to all-expenses-paid "symposia" at Caribbean resorts in order that they learn about the latest chemical creation. Wyeth-Ayerst, a drug manufacturing multinational, has been known to offer physicians frequent-flyer mileage for prescribing certain of their drugs. And of course most people are aware of the constant supply of gifts passed along to doctors by the drug salespeople. These are known in the trade as "reminder items."

But there are other promotional methods the drug companies employ on behalf of doctors that are not always so blatant or obvious. In a 1992 article entitled, "Pushing Drugs to Doctors," the American *Consumer Reports* magazine reported on how the drug companies often sponsor seminars at medical conferences where, unknown to attendees, the speakers are carefully chosen because of their known advocacy of certain drugs. Just as insidiously, the drug companies exploit the credibility of medical journals by paying for "supplements" that are piggy-backed onto regular issues of these publications. These supplements invariably appear in the same very sober-looking format which the rest of the journal employs, but are in fact little more than propaganda efforts designed to capitalize on the busy doctor's view of these journals as presenters of unbiased information. A September 1991 supplement to the *American Journal of Clinical Psychiatry*, for example, dealt with "selecting appropriate benzodiazepine hypnotic therapy," and was sponsored by Wallace Laboratories. Virtually every article in the supplement focused on favourable information concerning the sleeping pill, Doral, manufactured by Wallace Laboratories.

Clinical research is another area where the drug companies have long been able to find fertile ground for the promotion of their products—selectively funding certain projects, and sometimes just as selectively releasing favourable clinical data. But a 1989 article in *Pharmaceutical Executive* offered succinct evidence of just how underhanded the drug companies are prepared to be in achieving their monetary goals. The article related to so-called "Phase IV" studies, which are conducted after a drug has reached the market, supposedly in order to detect any side-effects. It noted that such studies are often "not intended to yield publishable results." Instead, the journal stated, some drug companies have been able to increase product sales by simply "involving large numbers of investigators." These doctors then increase their rate of prescribing simply "as a result of participating in the study."

Despite the obviously high level of education which doctors have, and the fact that many of them believe themselves to be essentially above persuasion by obvious or subtle means, research has clearly shown that all of the above methods applied by the drug companies have demonstrable effect. Simply put, they work, and too often they work to the financial and psychological detriment of the patient.

But doctors and drug companies are not the only ones to blame in our unholy rush to the prescription counter. We as medical consumers are often too passive and too ill-informed to play the type of role we should play in the conduct of our own health. Looking back on my own problems, I had to ask myself why, when I first encountered side-effects with the pills I was prescribed, I didn't simply stop taking the medication? Upon reflection, I knew why. First of all, I had never been prescribed a tranquillizer, sleeping pill or antidepressant in my life. I saw them as medicine, not drugs. I had no idea of their make-up, their side-effects; least of all could I imagine that they might actually cause the feelings I was experiencing. Perhaps more importantly though, I trusted the neurologist completely. Like many of my generation, I suffered from the "deified doctor syndrome," of which many doctors are aware. When the doctor spoke, I listened. What the doctor said to do, I did. I never thought to question him. I was too submissive, too silent, too scared to question his wisdom, to exercise my rights as a patient. Perhaps if I had done so, his improved understanding would have hastened my psycho-social rehabilitation.

My only reaction, as my life began to go off the rails, was to assume that there must be something wrong with *me*. And this being the case, I could handle it. After all I was Felicity. I had always coped. And so, for a long time simple pride kept me glued together, and nothing could induce me to admit, even for a moment, that I could not cope.

Lage Vitus, National Executive Director of the South African Federation for Mental Health has stated, "The solution to our mental health problems often lies within ourselves, and . . . the main task of the mental health worker is to facilitate the efforts of the *patient to find the solution* (italics his) rather than subject them to arbitrary experimentation without their co-operation." David Bayever, founder of Drug Wise: Pharmacists Against Drug Abuse (South Africa) has suggested a two-pronged approach: "Doctors need to be more aware of what they are prescribing to their patients. Pharmacists need to give relevant prescription information to the patient, thereby creating mutual responsibility." This essentially tripartite approach places the patient on an equal footing with everyone involved, generating a much better understanding of the problem. The more individual autonomy and mutual respect between doctor, patient and pharmacist, the less the likelihood that abuse will occur.

In writing this book, I knew that I would have to "come out of the closet," throw away my cloak of silence and face the stigma of mental illness head on. In reflecting upon my apprehension at doing so, I realized that the most difficult thing for me to regain, during the entire course of my recovery, was my self-esteem. After I joined the International Training in Communication club, for instance, it took me three months, with my sister sitting close to me, to pluck up the courage to fulfil my first assignment—to read the four-line ITC pledge aloud. Even the justification of being a victim of a doctor-caused (iatrogenic) illness didn't automatically restore my self-confidence, and obviously revealing myself as a former "mental patient" would undermine whatever degree of self-esteem I had been able to recover. Nevertheless, I was determined to tell my story, to let people know of the dangers of benzodiazepine mismanagement, and that there are other, alternative ways of dealing with anxiety or depression.

There is no doubt in my mind that my breakdown and institutionalization came about as the result of gross mismanagement of my case by the medical profession, particularly as regards the administration of mood-altering drugs. The depression which followed came about as the result of that institutionalization and the bizarre pharmaceutical "soup" I was immersed in. But depression, be it doctor-caused or not, is the awful problem it is for most sufferers precisely because depression is so little understood by the public at large, and to a frightening degree by the medical community itself. Depression is all about loss—loss of security, purpose, vision, hope, self-image—and this loss cannot be measured on a scale. It is different for each person, as is the recovery. Today too many people still don't know that mental episodes and the healing of the mind do not follow a set pattern or time period. The mind is an unexplained phenomenon—how it heals is something doctors and researchers have been studying for years and are still not in agreement about.

The tragedy I have found with people dependent upon tranquillizers is that their coping skills (which may have been inadequate at the start) are now greatly diminished. I have watched grown men crumple, crying like babies, shaking their heads, wringing their hands, pleading and begging for something, anything, to reassure them that they are not losing their minds. Aside from having to deal with the problems which led them to pills in the first place, these people now have to face the added burden of coping with the symptoms of withdrawal. If they are not informed about the withdrawal symptoms, they may well be driven back onto the very pills they are trying to escape—a vicious circle.

We need to accept that it is perfectly normal to become anxious or depressed periodically. If it continues for more than a week, we need to acknowledge our problem and seek help. Genuine depression is not a figment of the mind. It is real and we need to face it. At the same time we need to know that it can in fact be treated, managed and cured. If, however, the first treatment option presented to you is medication, I'd like to suggest the following approach on your part.

Ask yourself certain questions. First of all try to *name* or pinpoint what is worrying, disturbing or frightening you. Having done this, *claim* responsibility for your feelings by asking what you can do about it. Having determined that, the final, crucial step is to *take* that action. Action is anathema to depression. It signals we are living in the present, the Now, the daylight. Resist depression's call to sloth, apathy and self-pity. Attack. Remove depression's teeth by action, any action.

Know also that depression waits at life's major crossroads for its victims, preying upon those devastated by death, retrenchment, divorce or major illness—any form of human suffering. But it is not the enormity of the event which triggers depression, rather it is our emotional response to it. When life is brought to a sudden standstill by events beyond our control, factors like fear, uncertainty and decision-making enter the equation and determine the outcome. Times of crisis are when we are at our most vulnerable and where the will, the spirit and the mind can be sucked dry. To prevent this from happening, it is imperative to communicate our feelings to someone. Sharing is always better than despairing. Done on a regular basis, the natural build-up of emotional toxic waste can be eliminated.

Although indiscriminate in its choice of victim, depression has some preferences—for instance people who are constantly looking over their shoulders, reliving the past. Nothing satisfies depression's inordinate desires more than watching people pull at their own innards—their regrets, mistakes and guilt. Without these ignoble remnants to feed on, depression will soon starve.

Just as often depression likes to attack the demanding "I want it now!" people. If you are one of those people, someone subject to intense highs and lows and periodic eruptions, you need to know that stress and pressure can be considerably reduced if you become aware of your own emotional switchboard. Ask yourself some questions: What or who is bothering me? What can I do about it? Am I reacting sensibly or going overboard? Try to understand the situation you're in. If you are prepared to give yourself time to take a breather, cool out, go for a walk, often things will resolve themselves. Observation and reflection will give you the answers. In doing this you may find, as I did, that some of our emotional pain is brought on, or strongly influenced, by how we are thinking at the time.

It took me a long while to realize how powerful thoughts are, and the integral part they play in one's ongoing mental health. When my thoughts raced off here, there and everywhere, I learned to bring them back by asking myself every conceivable question about what I was involved in at the time, whether that was sewing at the machine or scrubbing a potato. In this way I relearned to concentrate and focus. If I woke up thinking "today is going to be lousy," I learned that inevitably it was. Once I realized that I became introspective and self-judgmental in the company of negative people, and that whichever thought I allowed to dominate would win the day, I became conscious of the company I was keeping, and of what I was thinking. With practice it became habit to obstruct and squash negative thoughts before they could begin to harm me. I learned to feed my mind the morsels of small victories won and enjoy the feedback. I set myself little targets daily. I awoke to the rising sun every day with my humble today-I-will-do-it list. Whether it was answering a letter, visiting a friend, drawing up a new budget, sitting in a quiet spot reflecting on current events, I did it. Consciously.

Not all anxiety is harmful. Moderate amounts of anxiety often enhance our performance, and treatment should only be considered when the anxiety is out of all proportion to the stressor, when it is continuous, or when it impairs normal activities and functioning. Many anxious people will respond to an array of nonpharmacological remedies just as well as they will to any form of drug treatment. Simple changes in lifestyle, like more exercise or dietary alterations (such as giving up caffeine), can be enough to make modest degrees of anxiety perfectly manageable. Learning particular relaxation techniques has been enough to keep some anxious people functioning effectively. As well, traditional and more contemporary forms of "insight-oriented therapy"—dialogue with a trained counsellor or psychiatrist—has proven to work as well or better than drug treatment for people with mild to moderate anxiety. I know that in my case, simply communicating to anyone, never mind a counsellor, about my experience proved immensely helpful. When I started talking, hesitantly at first, about my experience to outsiders, it proved cathartic. It confirmed for me my wholeness, and restored my self-trust.

The crux of the matter with all these techniques is that we as potential patients must learn to more often look inward for our solutions, to our own resources, rather than outward, to doctors and pills. We have to avoid the tendency to demand the "quick fix," and we must never unquestioningly accept whatever any health-care practitioner tells us. We have to look for cognitive and spiritual answers that do not require the ongoing ingestion of pharmaceutical chemicals.

One of the problems that leads to prescription pill abuse is the fact that most health insurance plans reimburse poorly for psychotherapy, as compared to traditional pill-dispensing medicine, and this is something which needs to change, something that we all need to lobby to change. Without the kind of expensive publicity that the drug companies can put behind their products, nondrug approaches have received far less attention than they deserve.

Obviously it can be appropriate, in times of acute stress, to take a benzodiazepine. And if you are already taking such medication I would not advise that you desist or even reduce the dosage without first informing your doctor. Nor would I suggest that you take my singular frame of reference as a solution. I would suggest, however, that before you run off to a doctor you take a little inner journey. You may be surprised to find that the solution to your problem lies within your own power, within the strength of your own heart and mind. Drugs should always be a last resort, never a first one.

If you do choose to take a benzodiazepine, I'd strongly suggest that you take it at the lowest possible dosage, and for the shortest possible time. Even a few weeks of daily ingestion can lead to dependency. Question your doctor closely about how long you are expected to take the medication and exactly how you are to withdraw from it and what to expect. Don't hesitate to ask your pharmacist to show you the data sheet for the drug prescribed; this should indicate clearly what is known about the drug. Recall, if you will, my own example, where I never knew the rights I had as a patient. I never knew that I had the right to share in the decision and choice of therapy being suggested, that I had the right to know my medication, its duration, its side-effects and that I had the right to say no. And recall, in my case, the tragic consequences.

Sadly, too little has changed since my time inside the Institution. We still live within a kind of drug culture, where for far too many people pills are their first and only choice when they're confronted with emotional or psychiatric difficulties. A recent report on CNN stated that, as of March 20, 1995, "Forty-three percent of all Americans are on prescription drugs." A 1996 study co-authored by the clinical director of the extended care unit at Lions Gate Hospital in Vancouver, Canada, found that 27% of local seniors received at least one prescription for benzodiazepines in the preceding year. Twenty-seven percent! When questioned on the report, the director expressed little concern, pointing out that the figures "aren't that much higher than anywhere else."

Since about 1980, worldwide use of benzodiazepines has in fact levelled off, possibly even decreased, but the *overall* use of prescription drugs, has continued to burgeon, as the drug companies continue their successful strategy of introducing new "wonder drugs" and convincing doctors and the public of their value. The two most recent prominent examples are probably Ritalin and Prozac. More than one million American children now take Ritalin, an increase of two and a half times since 1990. A 1996 report by CTV, the largest private Canadian television network, cited the fact that "a growing number of doctors are now using antidepressant medicine [including Ritalin and Prozac] to treat children as young as six." There have been numerous disturbing reports within that country of high-school-age children breaking into the homes of Ritalin users, because the invaders want the Ritalin for their own intravenous use or for resale on the street as a kind of "poor man's speed." (Many prescription pills are notorious for their abuse on the street.) Prozac, the renowned "happy pill," was introduced by the Eli Lilly Co. in 1987, and has of course since then rocketed up the pharmaceutical best-seller list as a result of Lilly's strenuous promotional efforts, and a variety of reports issued by the medical community lauding its benefits. Ignored in all the hoopla was the fact that Prozac has been reported to induce irrational behaviour, including outbursts of murderous violence and suicide attempts. Very reminiscent of the Canadian report, in November of 1995 *The Sunday Independent*, one of South Africa's leading newspapers, noted that Prozac is being used to treat "a growing number of children [some as young as eight] even though it is not recommended for their use." It seems that in children, the drug companies have now found a new and as yet not fully exploited marketplace.

The great irony of my own situation is of course that drug side-effects and withdrawal symptoms led me and the doctors to believe that I was mentally ill—a phenomenon now recognized as "drug induced psychiatric disorder." My story is a cautionary tale about prescription drug abuse and mismanagement, and, unfortunately, it is anything but a unique story. In many ways mine is the proverbial happy-ending story, but as my story ends, thousands of other stories begin. Who will write the endings to these stories? Right at this moment, as you read these words, how many are on our highways, eyes glazed, hands gripping the steering wheel, accidents waiting to happen? How many marriages are breaking up? How many jobs are being lost? How many children are being neglected as their parents go through zombielike existences? How many elderly people are spending their twilight years in a drug-induced fog? How many students are being drugged into docile obedience with little understanding of possible consequences? It is an international tragedy, one of which most of us are totally unaware. But the sooner society is made aware of the dangers of prescription drug abuse, and given facts and information on the recognition and treatment of depression and anxiety, the sooner this destructive power will be contained, and hopefully eradicated. My hope is that this book will make a small contribution to that much needed outcome.

APPENDIX

The following drugs are listed, with both generic and brand names, according to the disorder they are intended to address, either anxiety, depression or insomnia. Most names are taken from product labelling published in the 1995 edition of *Physician's Desk Reference*. This and other relevant information is also contained in *The PDR Pocket Guide to Prescription Drugs*, published by Simon & Schuster Inc. of New York.

Anxiety disorders

Generic Name	*Brand Name*
Alprazolam	Xanax
Bromazepam	Lexotan
Buspirone hydrochloride	BuSpar
Chlordiazepoxide	Librium, Libritabs
Clorazepate dipotassium	Tranxene, Tranxene-SD Half Strength
Diazepam	Valium
Hydroxyzine hydrochloride	Atarax, Vistaril
Lorazepam	Ativan
Mebrobamate	Equanil, Miltown
Medazepam	Nobrium
Oxazepam	Serax
Prazepam	Centrax
Prochlorperazine	Compazine
Trifluoperazine hydrochloride	Stelazine

Depression

Generic Name	*Brand Name*
Amitriptyline hydrochloride with Perphenazine	Triavil
Amitriptyline hydrochloride	Elavil, Endep
Bupropion hydrochloride	Wellbutrin
Desipramine hydrochloride	Norpramin
Doxepin hydrochloride	Adapin, Sinequan
Fluoxetine hydrochloride	Prozac
Imipramine hydrochloride	Tofranil
Nefazodone hydrochloride	Serzone
Nortriptyline hydrochloride	Pamelor
Paroxetine hydrochloride	Paxil
Phenelzine sulfate	Nardil
Sertraline	Zoloft
Trazodone hydrochloride	Desyrel
Trimipramine maleate	Surmontil
Venlafaxine	Effexor

Insomnia

Generic Name	*Brand Name*
Estazolam	ProSom
Flunitrazepam*	Rohypnol
Flurazepam hydrochloride	Dalmane
Nitrazepam*	Mogadon
Quazepam	Doral
Temazepam	Restoril
Triazolam	Halcion
Zolpidem tartrate	Ambien

* Taken from a pamphlet distributed by Patients Rights Advocacy Waikato Inc. New Zealand.

LITHIUM

Lithium, or Lithonate, is also sold under the brand names Cibalith, Eskalith, Lithotabs, Camcolit, Liskonum, Phasal and Priadel. The generic name for this drug is Lithium carbonate.

Lithium is not a benzodiazepine. It is, in fact, an inorganic substance which occurs naturally in food and water, and the medication is derived from certain minerals. This does not mean, however, that it is a natural substance which everybody needs, and it is therefore important to note that lithium is not given because people have a deficiency of this substance. It is used to treat the manic episodes of manic-depressive illness, a condition in which a person's mood swings from depression to excessive excitement.

The important thing to know about lithium is that if the dosage is too low, there will be no benefit; if it is too high there can be lithium poisoning. Patient and doctor must work together to find the correct dosage. The body does not break down lithium; it enters and leaves the body in exactly the same form. There is no evidence that lithium is addictive, but prolonged or too high a dosage can result in kidney damage. Other side effects of the drug may include discomfort, drowsiness, frequent urination, hand tremors, mild thirst, muscle weakness and lack of coordination, diarrhoea, and nausea. These side-effects will vary with the level of lithium in the bloodstream, and their risk increases when lithium is taken in conjunction with other neuroleptic drugs.

The author regularly conducts seminars on the topic of prescription drug use and abuse. Anyone wishing to learn more about the subject by attending a future seminar is welcome to contact the author at the address below:

Felicity Bielovich
P. O. Box 199
Brakpan
1540
Gauteng
R. S. A.